School Attendance and Truancy:
Understanding and Managing the Problem

Edited by

~~~~ and Patricia Stoll

PITMAN
PUBLISHING

PITMAN PUBLISHING
128 Long Acre, London WC2E 9AN

A Division of Pearson Professional Limited

First published in Great Britain 1995

© Pearson Professional Limited 1995

British Library Cataloguing in Publication Data
A CIP catalogue record for this book can be obtained from the British Library.

ISBN 0 273 61686 2

10 9 8 7 6 5 4 3 2 1

Typeset by Phoenix Photosetting, Chatham, Kent
Printed and bound in Great Britain by Bell and Bain Ltd, Glasgow

The Publishers' policy is to use paper manufactured from sustainable forests.

Contents

Part I
Understanding
the problem

1 Review of *Truancy in English Secondary Schools*

Peter Miller

Introduction

This chapter looks at *Truancy in English Secondary Schools*, a draft report prepared for the DfE by Dennis O'Keeffe et al. of the Truancy Research Project, University of North London, 1991–92. The draft report was published in June 1993.

Brief overview

This was the largest study into school truancy yet undertaken in England. The target group consisted of pupils in Years 10 and 11 during the school year 1991–92, with a sample which studied every fourth school (150 schools in all) in 20 LEAs. The main basis of the research was anonymous pupil questionnaires with some evidence from the heads of the schools being sampled. The results are therefore mainly based upon pupils' statements of their own behaviour and attitudes.

The incidence of truancy is shown to be greater than was believed by the schools and motivated to a considerable extent by factors within the control of schools.

The report takes a measure of the incidence of two types of truancy, blanket truancy (BT) and post-registration truancy (PRT). In the latter a distinction can be made between pupils leaving or not leaving the building. Most frequent was PRT cutting lessons. PRT leaving the building increased sharply in Year 11.

Findings of the report

Heads were generally co-operative and were aware of the problem. They did, however, consistently underestimate its incidence.

There was a rise of 11 per cent in Year 11 truancy as compared with Year 10. Overall, 30.5 per cent of the pupils had truanted at least once during the previous half-term. The corresponding figure for Year 10 pupils was 35.8 per cent. Some 8.2 per cent had truanted at least once a week (Year 11: 9.9 per cent).

Many indulged in more than one type of truancy—the largest category of truanting consisted of pupils who engaged in both BT and PRT. It is notable that a quarter of Year 11 pupils reported that they had cut lessons without leaving the building. The senior managers of many schools will probably be asking themselves where all these pupils hide!

It has to be borne in mind that all the figures are under-statements of the true problem as many potential respondents were absent at the time of data gathering—17 per cent of the total possible were missing—and it must be suspected that many of these were truants.

There were considerable variations between schools. Fourteen schools in the survey had truancy levels of 20 per cent or less; 23 had 40 per cent or more. About a fifth of the schools had less truancy in Year 11 than in Year 10 but this was not typical and in most cases there was considerably more—in fact over a fifth had double the amount. It is made clear, however, that most schools have a problem holding their pupils. Only 12 per cent of the schools had less than 25 per cent and only three per cent less than 20 per cent truancy.

There is a real problem here with significant numbers of Year 10 and 11 pupils missing school frequently—a very large loss in terms of educational and resource costs, especially in the case of the hard core of frequent truants. The authors of the study consider that tighter controls are likely only to affect occasional truants and are unlikely to influence the hard core. A more effective school ethos might drastically curtail both, they argue.

The *reasons* for truancy are explored in the study and the authors are able to demonstrate that the questionnaire answers show that institutional factors are more significant than pupils' home background. This is hopeful in that schools may be able to impact the problem, but the factors are complex and may be difficult to tackle.

There is very strong evidence of rejection of particular lessons. One in five of all pupils truant from particular lessons, quoting dislike of the lessons (especially on grounds of perceived irrelevance) or particular teachers. Teachers seen as unpleasant were the most alienating rather than those regarded as unhelpful or not interested. The wish to avoid certain lessons was the reason most frequently cited, this rising with more frequent truants. The subjects most often mentioned were PE and French.

Among the reasons for subject-specific truancy was the pressure of coursework; the authors suggest that more preparation for the demands of coursework might ameliorate the situation.

Other reasons for truancy which might have been expected to be significant such as illness, bullying and home problems were hardly mentioned by the pupils in this survey.

Evidence from the survey shows that truancy was typically social—that is, more often with friends than not—but not undertaken because of peer pressure.

The data suggests that schools were more popular socially than intellectually. The reasons for not indulging in truancy were about equally split between positive and minatory. There was no apparent fear either of the police or of the education welfare officer (EWO)! The main reasons given were that:

1. Parents might find out (48 per cent).
2. Pupils did not want to miss school (40 per cent).
3. The school might find out (38 per cent).

It is disturbing that 44 per cent of the truants say that their parents know what is going on and that truancy is seen to be easy by 46 per cent of them. This latter figure varied a great deal between schools.

School and parental influence can be shown to have an effect—those schools where pupils reported fear of being detected by the school or parents had lower truancy rates and vice versa.

The question of whether pupils liked school showed that 50 per cent of non-truants liked school and only 13 per cent disliked it—quite encouraging. Perhaps more surprisingly, however, most truants liked or at least tolerated school, with only 31 per cent replying that they disliked it. This question of liking or disliking school did not appear to affect schools' truancy levels.

School subjects were generally approved by the respondents, even truants, of whom 54 per cent said the subjects they studied were mostly useful (non-truants 72 per cent), and 75 per cent of truants said that at least half their subjects were useful (non-truants 92 per cent). Again, however, approval of lessons did not correspond to schools' truancy figures.

A large proportion of pupils, 75 per cent of non-truants and a surprising 58 per cent of truants, stated their intention to continue their education after Year 11 either at school or at college. This factor is linked to schools' truancy levels.

The foregoing factors lead the authors to suggest that schools with high truancy levels can improve attitudes and so attendance by:

1. Tightening up on controls.
2. Promoting an ethos which values education.
3. Identifying and improving areas of the curriculum affected by truancy.

The socio-economic environment as well as the institutional and managerial arrangement of schools affect levels of truancy. No regional effect could be detected but truancy was a little higher in inner cities than in mixed suburban/prosperous suburban areas. Areas which were described as exclusively prosperous suburban had lower levels again. A similar effect was detected with levels of entitlement to free school meals. Overall there was some 'poverty' effect, but it was not particularly significant on the data available. There was a much more significant link between socio-economic factors and attendance on the day of data-gathering. This may well, of course, indicate that there were high levels of BT in deprived areas, but the case is not proven.

Levels of truancy reported by boys and girls were similar overall, but truancy by boys climbs steeply in Year 11. Single-sex girls' schools had lower truancy; county schools slightly higher than non-county schools. Age-range and size of schools made no discoverable difference.

The authors point out that there are startling variations in truancy levels between the 20 LEAs in the survey, from 25.3 per cent to 38.8 per cent. These variations are not related to region or to socio-economic levels. In fact the best three LEAs were in notoriously depressed areas.

An attempt is made in the report to grapple with the school ethos factor. Heads or their delegated form-fillers when describing the ethos of their schools 'tended to converge in repetitive affirmations of virtue'! This made it difficult to establish any link between truancy levels and ethos of individual schools. The question of ethos is, however, clearly linked to the importance reported above of parental and teacher awareness and action; perceived school vigilance can be effective in reducing truancy levels.

Truancy league tables

Since the report appeared, the Secretary of State for Education has announced (3 September 1993) that truancy league tables for individual primary schools are to be dropped, but are still to be published for secondary schools. He has also asked OFSTED to make a special study of how truancy is being dealt with in a sample of schools.

The report itself is politely reticent on the subject of these league tables. It is not easy to see how these could have any positive impact upon what is undoubtedly a significant issue. What schools can do is to draw upon the evidence contained in this report as they draw up their own strategies to tackle truancy.

Note

Published with the kind permission of Croner Publications. © Peter Miller, 1993.

References

O'Keeffe, D.J. (1994) *Truancy in English Secondary Schools*, HMSO.

2 Understanding the problem: truancy and curriculum

Dennis O'Keeffe and Patricia Stoll

Introduction

This chapter tries to outline the anatomy of what we know about truancy in English secondary schools, in particular highlighting the curricular determinants of the phenomenon and seeking to understand these further. It also considers the reasons for the deep reluctance of so much of officialdom to recognise the truth about this grave inadequacy in the curriculum.

The centrality of the curriculum

Intuitively one guesses that the last thing any conceivable British government would like to hear today is that truancy and attendance turn more than anything on the popularity/unpopularity of various subjects in the curriculum. After all, hundreds of millions of pounds have been spent since the late 1980s getting the National Curriculum into place. No conceivable Labour government is likely to oppose the National Curriculum—education is very much Labour's patch and the National Curriculum is so appealingly socialist an idea.

   In general we may also say that the educational establishment is also pro National Curriculum and thus not disposed to regard truancy as a curricular matter. By 'educational establishment' we mean the assorted group of senior civil servants, inspectors, union bosses, educational professoriat, teacher educators and educational journalists who collectively make up the non-elected governance of education. Initially this establishment—with the exception of the civil servants who planned the National Curriculum—was hostile, but soon declared itself in favour of the innovation, it being the proposed testing of schools and their being sorted out into performance rank order which offended some of the teacher unions, for example. The bureaucratic centralism of the proposals, by contrast, has passed without a murmur of real dissent in the Inspectoral services, the teacher unions, the ranks of teacher educators, and so on.

It is probably fair to say that a massive array of interests now sees itself as standing to lose status and credibility from public recognition that the curriculum is even a partial failure.

Yet the DfE publication *Truancy in English Secondary Schools* (O'Keeffe, 1994) has shown, on a huge scale, that the main engine of truancy in our secondary schools is the curriculum itself. The same result, drawing on a more limited empirical base, was shown by Patricia Stoll's fieldwork in the 1980s, jointly presented with Dennis O'Keeffe under the title *Officially Present: Post-Registration Truancy in Nine Secondary Schools* (Stoll and O'Keeffe, 1989).

Indeed, an interesting sidelight is thrown on the question of the relation between conceptual, reflective writing and empirical research by the consistency between *Officially Present* and *Truancy in English Secondary Schools* on the one hand, and the much earlier *a priori* essay by Dennis O'Keeffe, published in 1981 under the heading 'Industry, truancy and the school curriculum' (Flew et al., 1981). The author then reasoned that if there were large-scale truancy, as so many of his postgraduate students stressed,[1] and if the curriculum were the main business of school, then the two issues were quite likely to be intimately related.

The course of O'Keeffe and Stoll's subsequent research has seemingly shown the irresistible truth of this modest assumption. It would seem that if an issue is thought through sensibly, it is quite likely that empirical inquiry will bear it out.

In the event, O'Keeffe's 1994 report can be taken as having shown the enormous influence curriculum seems to have on the willingness of teenagers to be in school or class. It is a very big and demonstrable influence which dwarfs any other causal variable in the determination of truancy.[2]

The report has not shown that children do not like the curriculum in general. On the contrary, it has shown that they do.

It is rather that a very large number of children do not like some of their lessons. This fact, which the educational establishment seems to find so unpalatable, is the key to understanding truancy in English secondary schools.

Sociology, not psychology, is the proper tool for analysing truancy

It is well known that in many educational contexts during the last 50 years, sociological insight has, bit by bit, been ousting psychological understanding as the principal investigative tool. The authors' work belongs broadly to this sociological tradition. This does not mean we wish to be associated with much of what has passed as sociological thinking on education in this country in recent decades. Neither author has been influenced, for example, by the hateful neo-Marxism which so disfigured British sociology for all of the 1970s and some of the 1980s. Nor does there seem to us much genuine educational mileage to be found in the study of French antinomian thought of the Foucault variety.

At least we were at one with the 'new' sociology of education, however, in regarding traditional psychology of education as quite inadequate to the study of some aspects of children's behaviour at school. We took (and take) this to include truancy. No one would deny the importance of deficiencies in children which have their origin outside school, though in this case, too, sociology is often the appropriate tool for intellectual study. Nor do we deny that there are many personal characteristics of children which both impinge on their learning and defy sociological examination. We are not disputing that psychology has its place in the study of school-children.

At the same time it has always seemed to us absurd to overlook those factors which lie within the culture of the school itself and therefore by definition belong to the sociological realm of investigation. In particular we think that to neglect so important and variable a phenomenon as the school curriculum itself is inevitably to leave out a large part of the story. Indeed, insofar as we fail to consider school-based factors, we end up precisely with the fatally flawed psychology of years ago, which viewed school as an unproblematic good and anyone who recoiled from it as *ipso facto* deficient, or deviant or even protocriminal (Tyerman, 1968). Sad to say, this outlook is still apparent among many politicians and administrators. Either they regard children as possessing a disfigured psychology, or, if they do take a sociological perspective, this is so solely in relation to children's bad homes etc.

Such perspectives are not so much false as deeply partial. In particular, as we have suggested, they tend to promote the view that school is wholly unproblematic so that any children not finding it so must in some way be thought of as themselves problematic and inadequate.

The outline of the north London study

The Truancy Unit's 1994 DfE study (O'Keeffe, 1994) revealed that school influences, the overwhelming majority of which were broadly describable as 'curricular', dwarfed other influences in the explanations given by truants for their truancy. Dislike of school as such was far less potent a factor in generating truancy than curricular disgruntlement. Since the detailed data is presented elsewhere in this book, let us confine ourselves to the barest outline of our results.

We conducted research into pupils in Years 10 and 11 in the winter of 1991–92. Of nearly 38,000 students surveyed, about a third admitted truanting at least once in the previous six weeks.

Within this statistic lie other more dramatic ones. Among 16-year-olds, ten per cent of all pupils said they were truanting at least once a week. It was not, therefore, a case of lots of people doing it a little and rather few doing it a lot. There was also a big jump of more than ten per cent between the two years. Subsequent commissioned research by the authors also shows that truancy is a rising function of secondary education.

The distribution of truancy among types is also very revealing. We looked at two main forms of truancy: blanket truancy (BT) and post-registration truancy (PRT). Most truancy is PRT rather than BT, though most truants do both. Most PRT does not even involve leaving the building. Most significant of all, lesson dissatisfaction greatly surpasses all other influences in the determination of truancy. Two-thirds of truants say they truant for this reason among others and one-fifth say this is the only reason they ever truant. No other single reason compares. For example, dislike of school is a rather small cause of truancy, at least as a separate influence. Only five per cent of truants cited dislike of school as a sole reason for truanting. Indeed, our findings show that school is generally popular and accepted. While most students, and even most truants, accept most of the curriculum, the school is even more accepted by the generality of children.

The questionnaire yielded other reasons pupils truant. We know there are home influences which affect school performance significantly. Some of the truants say so, though far fewer than those who say they dislike some lessons. Some truants speak of being cold and depressed. Of course, there are causes involved in truancy which we cannot get at, because children either do not say what they are or cannot articulate them. We are probably looking at intellectual and social inadequacies built up over years, some of which are transgenerational. None of this reflection can detract, however, from the brute fact that, asked in confidence why they truanted, children cited lesson-dissatisfaction as much the most important reason.

Assorted underestimates

We should stress that our results are very much underestimates. First, we missed more than 7,000 students. Having aimed at 45,000, we in fact got just under 38,000. We presume that the missing children must have included a high proportion of frequent truants, unable to report on themselves, because they were up to what we had hoped to ask them about.

Next, we asked the students about a small time-period—the half-term previous to their filling in the questionnaires. This 'research window' was willed on us by the civil servants, probably justifiably, since it does tend in the direction of 'homogeneity' of result. On the other hand, the earlier research headed by Stoll, asked Year 11 (at the time Fifth Year) pupils, how much they had truanted since they began their GCSEs, some 16 months before. She picked up levels of 70 per cent. This reflects two elements missing in the DfE report. One is an additional number of very occasional truants, engaging in the activity less than once a term. The other, more important, lacuna concerns the likelihood, available to common sense, that truancy tends to shoot upwards in the summer term.

Moreover, the huge absences which the report discovered in some schools probably conceal a very high level of unrecorded blanket truancy. Nor, though we did not find much proven influence of inner-city location on levels of truancy, can we claim to have investigated the inner-city problem thoroughly.

We can hazard a generalisation, however. The scale of the truancy we found, with the extreme likelihood that it is a considerable underestimate, in conjunction with the claims of truants that their activity is mostly a question of their disliking some lessons, suggests that we have on our hands an intellectual crisis. We repeat that this involves widespread rejection of particular lessons rather than of the curriculum itself. In other words, though alarming, the crisis has not yet reached a critical stage. What we have to guard against is that such a crisis, ignored or denied by the establishment, could if unchecked reach drastic proportions.

Three issues are appropriate for discussion in the remainder of this chapter:

1. Why certain subjects are unpopular.
2. Further discussion as to why the government, or educational establishment, should reject the authors' findings that some of the key subjects are very unpopular with large minorities of the pupils. Why does the DfE still largely ignore PRT, for example?
3. The nature of the intellectual confusion/crisis in education.

Why some lessons are unpopular

The most unpopular lessons are games/PE, French, maths and science. Children also truant from history, geography, and indeed, from every subject on offer. Subjects are variously unpopular because students:

- find them boring/irrelevant;
- find them too difficult;
- cannot keep up with coursework/homework; and
- do not get on with teachers.

Both kinds of truancy are more sensitive to questions of subject-dissatisfaction than to any other influence, though PRT is more sensitive in this way than BT. Both forms of truancy are more sensitive to lesson-dissatisfaction at higher levels of frequency than at lower. The inference drawn from these findings is that children do indeed see the curriculum as the real business of school and that a sizeable number are dissatisfied with some of their lessons. This last finding relates to non-truants too. There are considerable numbers of non-truants who, when asked, expressed dissatisfaction with some of their lessons.

None of our findings means that truants reject most of the curriculum. Nor do many truants allege that teachers are technically incompetent. Our results show that most truants like or accept school and most want to stay on after the minimum leaving-age. They see school in a less favourable light than do non-truants; but they are much less different attitudinally from non-truants than might have been supposed. Widespread alienation from school is not typical of the pupils in this country, as yet. But the positive dislike of some subjects is incontrovertible.

It is worth considering some of these in a bit more detail. Take games/PE. It is clear that about a third of our young citizens do not like games and PE. Why should they? Why does the games lobby insist on everyone's having to engage in competitive sport and why does the government give in to this lobby? Is it argued that competitive sport is crucial to civilisation? Why not allow more flexibility?

In a way, French is even more interesting. After the long struggle for global linguistic mastery, the winning side feels compelled to inflict the language of the losers on its own population. Why?

Maths, science and English are more important: all we get on these is fudge, and the pretence that we can splice irreconcilable opinions. In the crucial case of English, a universal curricular language for our part of the world, reforms have made the subject less popular than before. Patricia Stoll witnessed this very vividly in the 1980s at the school where she both worked professionally and also began her research. The burgeoning weight of coursework turned English, a popular subject in her school in the early 1980s, into a deeply unpopular one in the later years of the decade, associated with very high levels of truancy.

Why the DfE does not want to know

For whatever reasons truants act as they do, the DfE is almost totally ignoring the authors' results. No minister has seen fit or even seemed inclined to face up to the sports or the French lobbies. Moreover, the case of truancy seems one where for the most part the civil servants have called the tune. The main reasons for official reluctance to face up to the Truancy Unit's findings are easily listed:

1. Because the civil servants are in charge. This is not entirely true, since a forceful Secretary of State or minister can make a big difference; but contingently it is true enough to worry us. The British Civil Service is not corrupt and it is highly educated. We believe its policy influence is often wrong, however (viz the National Curriculum), and that it should not be making policy anyway.
2. Because the entrenched view at the DfE is that school is an indefinitely worthwhile good from which only a deviant would recoil. This is the old 'psychologism' of the interwar period. Would the civil servants still say this if they visited New York or Chicago, or if London or Manchester slipped into that level of school-rejection? Both ministerial pronouncements and the anti-truancy initiatives presumably devised by the civil servants still seem to assume that the truant is a nailbiting inadequate at best or at worst a potential criminal.

3. Because so much time, and so many resources and careers have been sunk in the National Curriculum. It is intolerable to the education establishment to admit that huge bits of it are not working. Let us repeat that it is widely believed, though hard to prove, that the National Curriculum was originally a civil service project, one which senior civil servants had been rooting for since the late 1970s. Nor, one has to add, does there seem to be anything untoward in the civil service view. It is almost certainly perfectly genuine. After all, lots of their fellow citizens also see the centralisation of curriculum as a good idea, as do the citizens of other free societies, such as France. We think the conception is wrong and that this error is something the free world will have to confront sooner or later.

4. Because it is too painful to think in terms of intellectual crisis. It is much easier to think in 'practical' terms about reorganising teacher education, or teacher 'training' as it is incorrectly—and usually—called. It is easier to centralise the official transmission of knowledge and culture than it is to confront the huge gulfs between the thinking of different authorities *vis-à-vis* English, mathematics, history, and so on.

5. Other elements in the educational establishment (for example, the leadership of the most powerful unions) share most of the civil servants' views and proceed to add some of their own. For them it is much more comforting to think our problems can be solved if we refuse to allow competitive ranking (except in games) or pretend that everything can be fixed if only enough resources are committed.

The likely results of refusal to face the evidence

We should note in any case that education decision-making is fractured. This is because the educational élite is not homogeneous. Most academics in teacher education and journalism originally opposed the whole concept of the National Curriculum. Opinion has shifted in its favour in the last five years. It is now the systematic assessment of what children learn that is the focal point of opposition to government education policy. The civil servants and the rest of the establishment now agree about the National Curriculum. Today it is over assessment that they fall out, since the civil servants want testing and the rest of the establishment does not.

Meanwhile, the government itself drifts. While it gives in to the games lobby's view that we must have competitive games, it also seems prepared to give in to the inconsistent view that we must not have competitive examination results published for all to see.

We can reasonably predict a continuing high incidence of truancy if we put these considerations together. Even after Dearing, the curriculum will continue to be too rigid and inflexible, with students forced to play football or netball etc. and to study 'French'. At the same time the intellectual output of schools will continue to be inadequately monitored. These circumstances make truancy on an increasing scale highly likely.

The intellectual crisis in education

There is space now for no more than a relatively brief sketch of the thesis that there is an intellectual crisis in our civilisation. Nor can we do more than continue to adumbrate our opposition to that very un-British thing, the National Curriculum. It was not adopted because of its extreme similarity to Leninist bureaucratic centralism. But people should be apprised of this grotesque likeness. It is deeply to be regretted that it emerged under the Thatcher administration, a dispensation whose leader was notably sympathetic to the views of Hayek. Hayek would have rejected such a notion peremptorily, as a typical example of the constructivist error.

Future historians will reject this development as unworthy of, and unworkable in, a free society. It is not an idea or a system fit for a free people's intellectual arrangements. What is needed is competition and variety, not standardisation and uniformity. So far from constituting an answer to our intellectual problems, the National Curriculum, and the fanatical hostility to intellectual rank order which accompanies it, are symptoms of the malaise.

It is worth noting that the centralisation of decision-making, combined with a near total failure to evaluate outcomes, is the core of all bureaucratic centralism. The manifest failure of this combination everywhere it has been attempted should have ruled it out of court, especially in this country, where such large-scale and contradictory constructions have always been regarded with suspicion.

The failure of progressive education

A crucial background question is the secular influence of progressive education. By any standards it has been a massive failure; but its proponents continue to refuse to identify what might count as definitive evidence against it. The curricular impact is considerable, at least if it is true that progressive education has resulted in low standards of basic competence. The point is that if you are illiterate and innumerate, or even merely very incompetent in these regards, you cannot cope with the secondary curriculum.

It cannot be denied that in a free society some teachers will want to work under the progressive mode. Nor is it disputable that some parents will want this for their children. What is so appalling is that this mode has been imposed as common practice at the primary level and that the citizenry, who were never asked what they wanted for their children, have been for decades educationally disenfranchised.

Our hypothesis is that progressive education has resulted in low standards of basic attainment, unfitting many of those who have passed through its elusive benefits for the challenge of the secondary curriculum. We found that almost a tenth of truants in our recent survey said they found the subjects from which they truanted too difficult. It is an easy and reasonable step to the view that this implies an inadequate preparation, unless we also incline to the idea that these children are inherently incompetent. We incline, however, to the contrary view that most secondary children should be able to reach a decent standard at GCSE if they have been properly prepared. If they do not, this constitutes not a commentary on their academic potential but on their academic attainment, which should have been much better.

Furthermore, unpreparedness may be a significant factor in the common complaint by truants that subjects are boring or irrelevant, that they cannot keep up with the coursework or homework and that they dislike some of their teachers. Obviously the interconnections between such variables are both extra-ordinarily complex and very hard to measure. It seems inconceivable, however, that they do not so interconnect.

Progressive education in this country, however, is only part of the story. The entire western world is gripped by an intellectual crisis. Truancy is simply one of its indices.

The crisis has many components. There are inevitably huge international variations. For example, in the United States there has occurred a disastrous collapse of the literary aspects of the secondary curriculum. In this country such an outcome seemed a real possibility in the last few years, but a more traditional literary culture seems to be reasserting itself, if only tentatively.

Wherever it occurs, however, the crisis in part reflects the coexistence of incompatible views and preoccupations. First there is the contradiction between insisting that children be at school and resisting any idea of their being assessed on what they learn there. The first impulse here is managerial and paternalist; the second is romantic syndicalism. Compulsory education clashes even more with the idea of effectively letting children do what they like in the classroom, which is what progressivism amounts to in its more extreme manifestations.

There is a dysfunctionality about many schools, a looseness of purpose and discipline. Our survey, for example, shows that even children who like their lessons will truant if discipline is slack.

Strangely, along with this debilitating looseness, there is the belief that learning can be conceptualised in minute detail. For example, there are the technicist conceits of the National Curriculum itself. These rather forbidding ideas sit uneasily alongside the romantic child-centred hedonism of the progressive world-view.

Then there is the antinomian heresy of post-modernism, imported mainly from France in terms of intellectual gurus; and from America in terms of sub-political movements. This is a very powerful influence whose sociology has not been unravelled. One aspect of the crisis is widespread suspicion of the world. So ingrained is this among western intellectuals that some of their opponents have spoken of the 'hermeneutics of suspicion'. This is displayed in the propensity to see victims here, there and everywhere. If a sizeable minority of schoolteachers adopt these pessimistic views of the world, it will hardly make for a successful school environment.

Among many people in teacher education, for example, there is a hatred of the real world, which is seen as menacing and life-destroying, especially in its insistence on hierarchies and in its allegedly dehumanising impersonality. It is almost as if educators were saying that, at least in school, the horrid, competitive, anxiety-ridden world will be kept out. This view of the world is, we think, a huge and self-indulgent error. Competition is part of the life-blood of civilisation and the attempt to suppress it at school is disastrous. It will both lower standards at school and systematically misprepare children for the real world.

The mythology of race, sex and culture

We can get a direct handle on some aspects of the progressive view. For example, our data confirm our long-held view that too much is made by education in this country of prejudice in the areas of race, sex and culture. In our research we had about 12,000 truants. Not one said they 'bunked off' because of racist, sexist, or monocultural bias at school. These phenomena are more present in expert attitudinising than they are in teenage consciousness. It is also noteworthy that very few truants said they were subject to bullying.

We may put our critique of progressivism a little more formally.

So far from holding children in warm security, a soft, child-centred dispensation may, sometimes in the long run, sometimes immediately, encourage their truancy. It is a commonplace that children are often looking for the moral and behavioural walls when they are at school, and that they despise teachers who do not maintain discipline. Nor does this contention, that children prefer strongly disciplined schools, clash in the least with our contention that they essentially 'shop' their way through the curriculum, often truanting from curricular fare they deem not up to scratch. Children like school anyway, for obvious social reasons. They might well appreciate it more if it more closely approximated the severe world of adulthood. If we are right in this speculation, then progressive education is, indeed, deeply implicated in truancy.

Both present structures and present outlooks obstruct learning. The National Curriculum machinery, for example, diverts teachers from their proper duties, and resources from their optimal use. Teachers should transmit knowledge and values. We think most do this and most want to do it more effectively. How can they be really effective at it if they spend half their time filling in ridiculous forms?

We are not saying that it is easy to resolve our crisis; if it were easy to remedy it would not be a crisis. But certainly the National Curriculum has to go. We need a flexible curriculum and competing teaching styles if we are to meet the various needs of the young people in school. If we do not get these things right, then children will 'bunk off' from school, and even more from class, no matter how many resources we spend. And if we do not establish more effective teaching and social control in school, then truancy will get worse.

It is apparent that truancy has causes spanning the intellectual, the administrative, the psychological and the social factors. This is not surprising. Education itself is highly complex and controversial. There is deep disagreement among scholars and teachers as to its philosophical aims and socio-economic functions. Pupils can experience drastically different views of knowledge and discipline even within the same school.

Discontent could sometimes be much relieved by greater flexibility. There is huge truancy from games and PE and also from French, for example. Though there would be opposition, a policy for greater choice in games would help. As for French, it should be made completely voluntary.

Truancy may have a safety valve function, restoring equilibrium where it has been disturbed by lesson-dissatisfaction. We may be appalled at such a wasteful homeostasis and the illegality involved. Truancy *is* a gross waste of resources. We have not, however, thought through some of the implications of compulsory

education. Perhaps the debate should start now. How far should
we force children into lessons? In a free society, what are the
limitations on the legitimate use of coercion as a means of social
control?

On the limits of compulsion

The debate need not polarise between compulsion and purely
voluntary attendance; but do we really have to impose 11 years
on all children? The evidence on standards does not suggest that
these 11 years are always put to good effect. Patricia Stoll's
many years as a teacher have persuaded her that by Year 11, for
example, some students, particularly among the boys, have
simply outgrown school.

In any event, the long-run solution to truancy must involve at
its heart questions of the effectiveness of lessons. We cannot
entirely dispense with coercion in human affairs, and school-life is
no exception to this sociological law. Indeed, we have shown that
good discipline makes a larger apparent contribution to attendance
that does enjoyment of lessons. But we should try to minimise the
use of such coercion.

Even if the arguably Orwellian or nosey-Parker side of heavy
surveillance is exaggerated, we have to make school viable
intellectually. And, since it is a marked intrusion into adolescence,
it must be convivial. We will never get all fit pupils into all their
classes. If we want to reduce truancy, schools must be intellectually
effective, strict and yet welcoming. A difficult mix; but we must
achieve it if we want students at school for 11 years minimum.

The indispensability of proper examinations

Any debate on the curriculum for 14- to 16-year-olds—the age
group of the pupils in our official government sample—will
inevitably focus on the public examinations, for the two go hand in
hand. The curriculum during the final two years of compulsory
education is effectively determined by the public examination
system. This seemingly irresistible fact shows how unrealistic are
the principles of primary education insofar as they deny this public
imperative. Indeed, though we cannot pursue the matter more than
cursorily now, the interaction between primary education on the
one hand, and secondary and even tertiary on the other, is the great
unwritten theme of modern British sociology of education. We
have been witnesses to a conflict of irreconcilable claims about the
nature of learning and the ways in which it should be regulated and
assessed. The present authors see the failure of decades of

progressive primary education as the sad, unacknowledged intellectual void behind our pandemic present levels of truancy.

The battle has been essentially between the progressive and the traditional curriculum. It cannot remain in its present deadlocked stasis. It is a mark of success for the progressive aspiration that it has in part colonised the secondary stage. There is now a much restricted choice of examinations at 16 years. This is in line with the upward moving egalitarianism which has emanated from the primary schools. The fact that examinations remain so urgent in the outlooks of children in their last years of school, on the other hand, represents the failure of the progressive missionary recasting of secondary schools in the primary image.

All pupils in maintained and independent secondary schools follow *ipso facto* the General Certificate of Secondary Education (GCSE) courses in all subjects, irrespective of their abilities and aptitudes. So we are in a kind of half-way house between the rival philosophies. There are no alternative curricula at present. We propose that such choice be revived. Pupils in their examination years should be offered variety in curricula and examinations. We know of two schools, for example, which were offering excellent courses with a vocational dimension for pupils aged 14 and 15 who were not coping with the mainstream curriculum. Such courses were not validated by the then Schools Examination and Assessment Council (SEAC) because they were judged to be incompatible with the National Curriculum.

This is an example of the interests of pupils being sacrificed on the altar of pseudoequality. No one must be different; all must do the GCSE. All non-conforming courses must be closed. This reflects the continuing grip of socialist ideology on the organisation of schooling. Citizens in a free society would not tolerate such restrictions on the operation of ordinary commerce. It is only the long habituation to socialist coercion, which has bracketed education off from other aspects of economic life, which permits such restrictions to operate in the world of school.

To be fair, there is some element of choice between subjects for pupils in Years 10 and 11; and Dearing has rather improved matters in this respect. Nevertheless, on balance, since the advent of the National Curriculum, 'options' have been much reduced. Interestingly, this state of affairs does not apply to British pupils studying overseas. We have before us as we write confirmation from a teacher in a school in the Middle East that pupils in this school have a choice between the General Certificate of Education (GCE) 'O' level and the GCSE. Most pupils take 'O' level examinations; only those pupils of lower ability take GCSE, the examination taken by all abilities in England. It is hard to imagine that this would not be the public response here too if the choice were available. Why are our children being short-changed in this way?

Since the current examination system appears to be unsuitable for many of its clients—it fails to stretch the most able pupils and does not cater for the needs of the least able—it could well be that here is to be found the main cause of truancy among older pupils. Our findings have shown repeatedly that young people are not alienated from school *per se*. We have evidence, nevertheless, both from our large report for the DfE and from subsequent school-based research commissioned by LEAs, that truancy increases year on year. Our DfE research showed a 9 per cent increase in truancy by girls between Years 10 and 11 and an even higher, indeed dramatic increase—of 13 per cent—in truancy by boys. In the smaller LEA studies, there was a clear tendency for truancy to move upwards in every year of secondary education. Obviously this can vary with the schools concerned. Nevertheless, the general tendency for truancy to constitute a growing function of secondary education is so marked as to seem like an empirical law of secondary education.

For the children moving between Years 10 and 11, the explanation for the marked increase in truancy which occurs may be that many pupils are simply unable to cope with the work involved in GCSE examinations, because of either intellectual inadequacy or boredom with the subjects. They fail to meet deadlines and consequently fall behind with coursework. Nineteen per cent of truants in our DfE survey whose truancy is aimed at avoiding lessons gave difficulties with coursework as a reason.

Perhaps even more worrying is that the reason given by the greatest number of truants in this category (36 per cent) was the 'irrelevance' of lessons. It may well be that lots of boys and girls think that the lesson in question is simply not for them. We suspect that there is a link between the marked increase in truancy in Year 11 and the fact that many pupils are not entered for the final examination. There is little incentive for pupils to attend lessons if there is no examination at the end. It is not surprising that they start to truant. Furthermore, teachers may well turn a blind eye to such transgressions, preferring instead to concentrate resources on those pupils who are taking the examination. They may feel reluctant to expend a lot of time and energy pursuing what they perceive as a pointless exercise.

Obviously our thesis is that an improvement in primary and lower secondary education would markedly reduce truancy. We are not Utopians, however. No system will ever be truancy-free. However popular school may be we have to allow for the fact that a sizeable minority of teenagers are not going to enjoy much of the curriculum in whatever it may consist. What is reprehensible is that it is possible to see how truancy could be much reduced. Many children cannot handle an intellectual curriculum of the classical 'liberal' type. Forcing this on them results very often in truancy. At the same time our teaching often neglects instrumental essentials. This means that many young people leave school illiterate and innumerate. That many young people are unschooled in this basic way is itself another obvious source of truancy. The current education system, for all its unprecedented catalogue of recent reforms, still fails to address the needs of some pupils. Our failing to transmit universal literacy and numeracy in our young people short-changes both those who do aspire to liberal education and those who look for no more than basic competence in reading, writing and arithmetic.

The dire hostility to selection

If we were to identify the one phenomenon which we believe has led to our modern ills in the maintained sector, this would be the abolition of selection. The move to rid the education system of selection of any kind began with the abolition of the 11-plus examination. This ended the selection of pupils for grammar schools. The ending of selection in turn, as was foreseen and intended by its proponents, opened the way in due time for the demise of these institutions. This process itself proved surprisingly rapid. By the 1970s most grammar schools had gone out of independent existence.

The end of the 11-plus, then, 'produced' the new comprehensives. The relationship was not mechanical; nor did everyone view the new schools in a uniform light, Harold (now Lord) Wilson, for example, dubbed them 'grammar schools for everyone'. This, however, was not the view of their most ardent supporters, who, now that the grammar schools were gone, erected a new policy goal: 'mixed ability' teaching in the secondary school, to follow its ubiquitous triumph at the primary level.

We believe that mixed ability teaching has proved a failure both in its original primary home and in its adopted secondary one. Most secondary schools are now abandoning such disastrous arrangements for the teaching of academic subjects. Any kind of published academic ranking is anathema to much of the academic establishment and to some teachers. Nevertheless, the publishing of the academic league tables by the government does mean that no school can afford to experiment lightly with pupils' lives and risk unnecessarily poor examination results. We have ourselves observed schools which are serious about getting better academic outcomes abandoning mixed ability groups and reverting to teaching pupils in sets.

Perhaps the progressive experiment has run its course

It looks as if the progressive experiment has had its day. The departure from mixed ability teaching may well herald a new era, one in which schools are judged on their performance. It should not be claimed that the revival of teaching groups of broadly similar intellectual ability will in itself cure the ills of the upper school curriculum. We may take it that the problem is bigger than that. Nevertheless, this reassertion of earlier practice is certainly a step in the right direction. In any case, the progressive movement did more than influence pedagogical styles. It also effected, through the same 'egalitarian' inspiration, major changes in the curriculum and in the system of examinations.

Just as comprehensive schools replaced the tripartite system of grammar, technical and secondary modern schools, so the GCSE examination replaced the GCE 'O' level and the CSE. This meant that a differentiated system which formally recognised differing abilities was replaced by one which at the most recognised them as insufficiently important to justify separate examinations at 16-plus. Indeed, the GCSE was tailored to meet the needs of mixed ability teaching. In practice it was soon to manifest the same faults as the pedagogy which it reflected. It penalised both the able and the weak.

If educational dysfunctions such as truancy, bad behaviour and idleness, illiteracy, innumeracy and non-certification are to be addressed, then the curriculum for 14- to 16-year-olds needs to be changed radically. The National Curriculum, once seen as the panacea for all our ills, will, as we have argued, have to go. It is too coercive, too centralised, too prescriptive and too inflexible. We see no place for it in a free society. If anything it has exacerbated the problems of the upper school. Pupils' choices in subjects have been greatly restricted. Young people struggling with English are forced to study French. Self-conscious adolescents already compelled to run around hockey or football pitches are now, thanks to the games lobby, to find their misery intensified.

What is required is competition. We should have competition among schools and between examination boards. Parents who want a 'progressive' regime for their children should be able to find one. Those, we believe a majority, who want traditional academic subjects, discipline and academic competition, should likewise be free to seek these out. Variety and flexibility and as much choice as possible for parents and older children—that is the only way to get standards up.

Some have argued that our European counterparts may fare better than we, being in particular less nervous about selection than we are. We are not necessarily convinced that in France, for example, there is either more honest selection or superior average standards (Nemo, 1993). What is clear, however, is that without competition and selection, education is doomed to failure. It seems particularly reprehensible to require boys and girls to attend school and then subject them to years of inadequate teaching in some cases—and in the worst cases, to years of enforced egalitarianism—only to eject them into the labour market in many cases with useless intellectual credentials.

The critics of competition rightly allege that it has casualties. That is true: but all systems have casualties—not least our own comprehensive system if we are to judge it on the high levels of truancy and the numbers of pupils leaving school without qualifications.

Notes

1. Dennis O'Keeffe was at that time teaching part-time on the MA in Curriculum Studies at the University of London Institute of Education, where most of the students were teachers in London schools.
2. We guided our research informally by severe Popperian standards. To put the case formally, we hold, strictly speaking, not that we have shown definitively that truancy is a function of the curriculum, but that the evidence is highly consistent with that view. It is true that we expected to find this but we insist that had we found otherwise we would have held the hypothesis to have been invalidated.

References

Flew et al. (1981) *The Pied Pipers of Education*, Social Affairs Unit.

Nemo, P. (1993) *Le Chaos Pédagogique*, Albin Michel.

O'Keeffe, D.J. (1994) *Truancy in English Secondary Schools*, DfE/HMSO.

Stoll, P. and O'Keeffe, D.J. (1989) *Officially Present: Post-Registration Truancy in Nine Secondary Schools*, IEA Education Unit.

Tyerman, M. (1968) *Truancy*, University of London Press.

3 Truancy and the curriculum

Colin Coldman

Introduction

The debate on truancy is locked into sterile exchange of views on how to force or persuade absent pupils back into school. It is simply assumed that if pupils are present at lessons then all will be well. The problem of truancy begins and ends with absenteeism. Even the more sophisticated models of truancy, which acknowledge that truancy is a symptom of some deeper problem, concentrate on the problems the truant has (personal or social) and ignore the problems the school may have in offering and delivering an appropriate curriculum.

The author of the report *Truancy in English Secondary Schools* (O'Keeffe, 1994) deliberately set out to identify curriculum issues in the problem of truancy. The report revealed that truancy exists extensively throughout the upper years of secondary education in this country. Most reaction to the report has focused on this but has failed to take the debate on to ask: What can be done to persuade truants back to school? It is presupposed that the problem of truancy is primarily one of enforcement. All policy implications are taken to be structural—how can the system be tightened?, rather than pedagogic or curriculum issues—how can the school be made important to children?

As an immediate reaction this is natural enough. The scale of truancy is worrying and it is not surprising that the press should concentrate on this aspect of the problem and that the government should seek to reassure the public that measures are being taken to clamp down on truancy.

There is a considerable danger, however, that the debate will stop at this point and not progress to the more fundamental—but less sensational—issue of the relationship between curriculum and truancy. This chapter attempts to demonstrate using the data gathered by the University of North London Truancy Unit that the curriculum–truancy link is a strong one that needs to be urgently addressed if the underlying causes of most truancy are to be understood and countered.

Understanding the problem

The underlying assumption in most truancy studies is that truants are excluding themselves from something of great value. This is taken to be irrational behaviour resulting from such things as poor self-image, learning difficulties, problems with others pupils or lack of purpose. More general problems cited are unfavourable home background, psychological and behaviour problems and low intelligence. The solution is to reintroduce the truant to schooling and provide learning support. It is the emotional and intellectual problems of the child that need to be addressed so that the child can benefit from the good of education.

The TV-am factsheet 'Missing Out' summarises the assumptions of this truancy model. The truants become more prone to future unemployment and criminal tendencies because of their 'lack of concern for the importance of school-based learning'. They suffer from low self-esteem and this is reinforced by a 'lack of continuity of care in their lives and experience of failure and rejection'.

It is surprising with all the attention that has been given to student-centred learning that so little research has been directed at seeing the act of truancy from the truant's point of view.

It appears to be implicit that there is no good (i.e. rational) reason why pupils truant. But, by our changing the focus of truancy research, as has been done in *Truancy in English Secondary Schools*, a much richer model of truancy emerges, one which has far-reaching implications for educational policy.

The new assumption for truancy research proposed by the University of North London Truancy Unit is that truants may absent themselves from school for good reasons and that the aim of truancy research is to discover what these reasons are. The policy implications that flow from this model are considerably more expansive than has so far emerged.

Truancy as a measure of curriculum effectiveness

The report *Truancy in English Secondary Schools* revealed that truancy levels are running at 25 per cent for Year 10 students and about one in three for Year 11 pupils. This is not affected by the location or type of school, although it may be that truancy in inner-city areas is of a greater magnitude. The fact that so many children are truants was greeted with disbelief in some quarters of education.

This attitude is typified by Nigel De Gruchy, general secretary of the NAS/UWT, when he stated: 'the figures they (O'Keeffe and Stoll) quote simply do not reflect the reality we know exists in schools and classrooms. Classes are simply not that empty. Some pupils invent excuses for missing lessons like PE and then boast that they are playing truant.' (*The Guardian*, 1993.)

This attitude is revealing for two reasons. First, it shows a certain amount of contempt for the perception of pupils. Whatever the truth is about truancy it is not to be discovered by listening to the truants themselves. Second, it shows that Mr De Gruchy is locked into a preconceived notion of what truancy is and how it is manifested. What Nigel De Gruchy has not picked up on is the fact that pupils truant not *en masse* but in a sophisticated manner often absenting themselves for quite limited times and from specific parts of the curriculum. It was known before the work of the University of North London Truancy Unit that some pupils skipped individual lessons but there was no systematic attempt to measure the extent of this phenomenon or explore its importance as a measure of curriculum rejection. There are three major ways in which children may truant from the curriculum:

- Blanket truancy is a traditional type where pupils simply stay away from school.
- Post-registration truancy consists either of registering for a given session and then going missing or skipping individual lessons.
- In the case of post-registration truancy the truant may stay on the school premises or leave the premises.

These are the three major types of truancy, but before moving on to examine the impact of each type it is worth noting that these are not comprehensive. Pupils have many strategies for avoiding the curriculum, including for example obtaining teachers' permission for being elsewhere or extended visits to the toilet. In a badly organised classroom it is relatively easy for a pupil to be marked present at the beginning of the lesson but then skip the remainder of the lesson while the teacher is engaged in some other activity. The opportunities for absence are as wide as the pupils' ingenuity, which as anyone engaged in truancy research and most teachers will know is considerable. This point should not be overlooked by those who believe that electronic registration systems may be the answer to the problem of truancy.

It should also be noted that in the example stated above, where the pupil leaves the classroom after registering for one session, no record exists of the absence. Only the child and some of his or her classmates will know that the act of truancy has taken place. The teacher may subsequently discover the absence but this will not always be reported.

Teachers will naturally object to such descriptions of classroom life. The point, however, is that although this situation is far from typical, all teachers know that such classes exist and where they do truancy is likely to occur. First the opportunity is there, but more importantly the desire to be absent from such chaotic lessons does not appear unreasonable.

Educationalists can draw on their own anecdotal experience. Many classes are extremely well run, and the clear majority are organised in a satisfactory manner. But some are chaotic with little or no control and little recognisable learning taking place. It is these lessons that are likely to be the focus of the act of truancy as it is likely the act will not be recorded and the motive for truancy is self-evident.

Statistics and facts always need to be interpreted. One fact revealed by the survey for *Truancy in English Secondary Schools* is that overall 30 per cent of Years 10 and 11 pupils truant from school. The instant reaction to this may well be disbelief, as it was for Nigel De Gruchy above. The figures can not be this high— 'classrooms are simply not that empty'. If the school experience were uniformly good and truants were regularly absent from all lessons (the traditional image of the truant) this would be a valid objection. But it is precisely because this model has been supposed that truancy has largely been regarded as a marginal problem affecting only small numbers of pupils.

To explain the figure of 30 per cent truancy a new model of truancy is needed. Truants do not (typically) reject schooling as a whole but reject particular aspects of their school experience. They may therefore truant irregularly or regularly from chunks of the curriculum so that for the most part large-scale absenteeism does not take place.

It is unlikely that in any given lesson there is 30 per cent truancy. It is more probable that the 30 per cent who truant spread their truancy throughout the curriculum but concentrate on those lessons where the opportunity for truancy is present and the motive for truancy (i.e. the curriculum not meeting student needs) is strong. With this model of truancy as a rational act directed largely at parts of the curriculum it is possible to interpret the statistics of truancy in a more informed manner.

The implications of blanket truancy and post-registration truancy

Truanting from whole school sessions is the most blatant, least sophisticated form of truancy. This will often mean getting caught although some students can avoid this by feigning illness, forging notes or taking advantage of lax registration systems. Although this type of truancy is what truancy is traditionally taken to be, it constitutes only a minority of all acts of truancy. Twenty-three per cent of pupils truant by missing whole school sessions but only three per cent exclusively by this means. About 28 per cent of Years 10 and 11 truants never truant in this way.

If truancy were looked at exclusively through the phenomenon of blanket truancy (as is traditional) it would appear that truancy is a relatively minor problem. It is only when the less well recognised, but more frequent, phenomenon of post-registration truancy is added in that truancy reveals itself as being widespread.

Post-registration truants go missing following periods of registration or they skip individual lessons. The fact that this type of truancy not only exists but is more common than blanket truancy immediately suggests that truancy is much more closely correlated to curriculum and its delivery than has been previously recognised.

Why do many pupils choose to be absent from very specific parts of the curriculum? There is no one simple answer to this question. But it seems clear that the evidence gathered for *Truancy in English Secondary Schools* is that pupils do critically evaluate the quality of the curriculum delivery and are in many cases inclined to avoid parts of the curriculum that are perceived to be of little use or not properly delivered.

Both blanket truancy and post-registration truancy provide evidence of curriculum problems. But post-registration truancy is the more sensitive measure of this and the most common type of truancy. Seven per cent of truants truant exclusively after registration or by skipping lessons compared to three per cent for blanket truancy. Most truants practise both forms of truancy but post-registration truancy comprises the larger proportion. About 15 per cent of all truants go absent after registration or cut lessons several times per week. This type of truancy may well go undetected or officially unrecognised and again it should be stressed that these pupils will not all miss the same lessons.

In any given lesson the number of truants will usually be quite small—it is the cumulative truancy across the curriculum that is sizeable. The division and frequency of the various types of truancy are shown in Tables 3.1 and 3.2.

Table 3.1   Percentage of pupils who truant by type of truancy

Blanket %	Post-registration %	Blanket only %	Post-registration only %
23	28	3	7

Table 3.2   Form of truancy

	Blanket %	Skip lessons %	Register then truant %
Truant at some time	72	87	41
Truant once a week or more	15	21	10

Base: All truants

It can be seen from the above that registering and then truanting is not so common as other types of truancy but skipping lessons is the most common with nearly 90 per cent of all truants using this method of truancy at some time and over 20 per cent skipping lessons regularly. Blanket truancy is also common but not as common or frequent as skipping lessons and considerably less so than post-registration truancy in its combined forms. Blanket truancy still accounts for a large proportion of all truancy, which might suggest a widespread rejection of school as an institution rather than specific parts of the process of schooling. An examination of the reasons given for truanting in both major forms, however, suggests that curriculum dissatisfaction is a dominant reason for truanting.

Why pupils truant

In summary, truancy can be broken down into two main types—blanket and post-registration truancy. Of the two types blanket truancy is the one that is most readily recognisable and it is natural to think that this total boycott of school represents a complete rejection of school as an institution.

In fact, the evidence presented in *Truancy in English Secondary Schools* suggests that this is the case only in a relatively small minority of cases. Only about one-third (35 per cent) of truants who engage only in blanket truancy stated that they truanted because of a dislike of school. Most of these pupils (40 per cent) stated that they truanted in order to avoid particular lessons and 39 per cent gave other reasons for truanting. Further analysis of the reasons given by these blanket truants for their truancy provides still stronger evidence that most truants are not completely alienated from school as a whole. Only eight per cent of blanket truants gave avoiding school as the only reason for truanting even when this was the only form of truanting they engaged in.

Many give a mixture of reasons, of which avoiding school is only one. However, when asked to explain further why they wanted to avoid school many truants indicated curriculum-related reasons for missing school. There is no strong evidence, then, even among those pupils whose behaviour would seem to indicate a complete rejection of school, that there is widespread discontent with school as an institution. Indeed, it appears that many of these blanket truants are taking radical measures to avoid particular parts of the process of schooling. Thirteen per cent of these pupils missed whole school sessions solely in order to miss a particular lesson or lessons.

If we interpret the resort to blanket truancy alone as a crude form of truancy, then we may see post-registration truancy, because of its potential for the avoidance of sanctions, as the more sophisticated exercise. The evidence provided by those pupils who truant only after registration or by skipping lessons strengthens further the suggestion that truancy is strongly correlated with curriculum.

Of these truants 30 per cent want only to avoid lessons and 68 per cent truant partly or exclusively to avoid lessons whereas only 4 per cent do so solely in order to avoid school and only 27 per cent partly to avoid school. Only in two extreme cases do pupils truant exclusively through one mechanism, either only BT or only PRT. However, most truants engage in *both* types of truancy at various times. Again when the evidence of these truants, and truants as a whole, is taken into account the indication is that the truancy–curriculum link is strong.

Just under one-half of all truants (49 per cent) stated that they truanted, among other reasons, to avoid school, which initially would appear to suggest the view that truancy represents a complete rejection of the school as an institution. When they were invited to expand on this, however, it became clear that most of these pupils boycott school in order to avoid particular aspects of their educational experience rather than the totality of it. The relevant question asked of pupils was 'In the last half-term have you ever not come to school when you were supposed to, or left school after registration because you did not like school?' Pupils who answered yes were then given an opportunity to explain their answer. Although one-half of truants gave dislike of school as one reason for truancy only 23 per cent of these truants (i.e. 11 per cent of all truants) went on to say school was generally boring or oppressive. In other words, only about one in ten truants gave the response which would best fit the traditional view of the truant as being alienated from the whole process of schooling.

Many more of this group of truants (those claiming they wanted to avoid school) were able to give specific reasons why they wanted to miss school. Twenty per cent stated that they disliked a particular lesson or lessons and 27 per cent disliked a particular teacher or teachers (10 per cent and 13 per cent) disliked school because the work was too hard, suggesting a serious mismatch between the school curriculum offered and a perceived need of the truant.

Generally, truants appear to be disaffected not from school or the curriculum but from particular parts or experiences within the process of schooling. Two-thirds (67 per cent) of all truants truanted in order to avoid a particular lesson. Some of these pupils only truanted to avoid one lesson and many truanted to avoid several lessons but it is rare for any given truant to want to miss more than three lessons.

Although some lessons are less popular than others there is a wide spread of lessons which are prone to truancy. This again suggests that typically the number of pupils truanting from any given lesson is small but allows for the cumulative effect across the whole curriculum to be substantial. It is when the reasons for subject truancy are examined that the truancy–curriculum link becomes most apparent. Pupils are not vague in ascribing reasons for their dislike of particular lessons but are able to give quite specific reasons for their tendency to truant from these lessons. Thus, 36 per cent of these truants stated that these lessons are of no relevance to their lives. They were also able to indicate exactly why the lesson was disliked, with 29 per cent indicating that it was the teacher who made the lesson unattractive and 22 per cent stating that it was the subject matter that was unappealing.

Truancy and the curriculum

If truants were typically truanting from the school instead of particular parts of the curriculum then their absenteeism from each subject would be uniform. In fact some subjects are clearly more prone to truanting than others although no subjects are immune. Some subjects have low numbers of truants mainly because they are options studied by relatively low numbers of pupils. When this is allowed for, however, the two subjects most commonly truanted from are PE/games and French.

PE/games has the highest incidence of truancy. Of all pupils who truant at some time, 34 per cent truant in order to avoid this subject.[1] Clearly this indicates that this subject is particularly unpopular among a sizeable group of pupils although it should also be recognised that this subject provides increased opportunity for truancy through forged sick notes, parental compliance in providing excuses and off-site provision of the activity.

French is easily the second largest target for selective truancy. Twenty-seven per cent of all truants who studied French direct their truancy at this subject. This must raise a serious question about the viability and desirability of demanding the study of this subject by children who may be less than proficient in their own language. Other languages do not score so highly in terms of truancy levels, perhaps because if students are compelled to study a modern language it is likely to be French.

The other main subjects such as English, maths and science all have levels of around 18 per cent or 19 per cent (of pupils who truant) with other subjects such as technology and geography scoring slightly less at 16 per cent. Some subjects such as art have very low truancy levels.

Even on a national scale, then, there are clear curriculum implications of high truancy levels in particular subjects. However, for individual schools the truancy levels for individual subjects can vary enormously. In some schools a majority of pupils who truant will truant to avoid a particular lesson. Often this will vary from Years 10 to 11. The evidence of other studies conducted by the University of North London Truancy Unit suggests that this can also vary within year groups and affects particular subject sets. In other schools particular subjects are uniformly unpopular.

There can be little doubt that knowledge of the pattern of subject truancy is something that could assist schools greatly in detecting problems in the curriculum. Subjects that are uniformly unpopular across a year group or several year groupings suggest a structural problem in curriculum delivery. Where the truancy is focused on individual class groupings it may suggest a problem in the delivery of the curriculum for that particular group although it may also be caused by lax monitoring systems.

Truancy and the process of education

There is no real evidence that most truants are particularly hostile to the concept of education. On the contrary when specifically asked most truants endorse education as something to be valued. Fifty-eight per cent of all truants stated that they definitely wanted to continue their education after they were free to leave school (compared to 75 per cent of non-truants) and just 18 per cent said they definitely did not want to continue (8.5 per cent for non-truants). Clearly some truants are alienated from the educational process (as are a smaller number of non-truants) but most are not.

A similar result was shown when students were asked about whether they found their subjects useful or not. Fifty-four per cent of truants stated that all or most of what they learned would be useful and this figure climbed to 78 per cent for a half of what was learned being useful (non-truants scored higher at 71 per cent and 92 per cent respectively). As might be expected, truants are less enthusiastic about the utility of the curriculum than non-truants, but most still endorse the benefits of the majority of the curriculum offered. Nor is school a miserable experience for most truants although it is for a sizeable minority. One-third of all truants (33 per cent) stated that school was mostly or always enjoyable and another one-third were neutral. The remaining third stated that it was mostly or always unenjoyable.

As with all these figures, the national figures mask a sizeable range of responses for individual schools. Again, if individual schools were aware of their truants' attitudes on the utility and enjoyability of the curriculum, then curriculum reform might be able to follow.

Conclusion

In conclusion the statistics gathered for *Truancy in English Secondary Schools* suggest that measuring truancy can provide an important indicator of curriculum acceptance or rejection. Previously it had been largely assumed that truancy was a problem in itself and the only point of studying truancy as a phenomenon was to solve the problem of truancy, that is to get truants back to school. Truancy, being seen as deviant behaviour, tended to be looked upon as a relatively minor problem.

The work of the University of North London Truancy Unit suggests a much more important reason for studying truancy. Truancy is engaged in by a large minority of pupils. They do not typically absent themselves from school for long periods of time but are much more likely to focus their truanting on a particular lesson.

Typically truants are also quite clear about why they truant. The school as a whole is not usually rejected but parts of the curriculum are and for reasons that truants are quite capable of articulating. In other words, truants avoid school or bits of school for rational reasons. They perceive, rightly or wrongly, that parts of the curriculum offered are of no benefit to them and take a reasoned decision to miss that part of their schooling.

Instead of seeing the truant as deviant, then, we should be looking to truancy as an indicator of where school is failing. Studies by the University of North London Truancy Unit do not generally indicate that schools are failing completely as institutions although this may be true in those schools that have very high levels and frequencies of truancy. Truancy is a very sensitive measure of curriculum rejection. It can indicate, for any given school or for schools generally, what parts of the curriculum are being rejected. Truants can indicate where the curriculum problems are and what is the nature of these problems.

The truant is not only alienated from parts of the curriculum but is prepared to take rational and practical action to alleviate this disaffection. There can be no stronger indication of pupils' perceptions of where the curriculum breaks down than truancy. It is imperative that attention is shifted away from forcing truants back to school to attempting to understand the underlying reasons for truancy. Schools should treat truancy as a direct measure of curriculum effectiveness.

Notes

1. All figures are adjusted to allow for numbers of pupils studying each subject.

References

The Guardian (1993) 26 June.
O'Keeffe, D.J. (1994) *Truancy in English Secondary Schools*, HMSO.
Sheridan, S. (Ed) (1990) 'Missing Out', TV-am, October.

4 Truancy in a single secondary school

Martin Smith and Bob Ford

Introduction

The Hertfordshire School Attendance Project, a partnership between the Education Welfare Service and two designated secondary schools, was established in March 1993 with the aid of DfE–GEST funding. The objective of the Project was to identify, develop and disseminate good practice in promoting regular school attendance and to devise and implement strategies for improving levels of attendance at the designated Project schools.

An essential first step in this process was to identify accurately rates of truancy, post-registration truancy and parentally condoned absence at the designated Project schools. One of the ways we went about doing this was through a pupil survey. In this chapter we explain how we carried out this survey, what we learnt from it and the picture of truancy that emerged. For the sake of convenience and simplicity we will confine our explanation to just one of the designated Project schools.

Francis Combe School

Francis Combe School is a mixed comprehensive with a Year 7 to 11 population of 527 and an additional 80 pupils in Years 12 and

13. Around eight per cent of the pupils are from ethnic minority families. Forty teachers are assisted by several peripatetic music and specialist support teachers. The school is LEA-maintained and is operating in an environment in which most of the neighbouring schools are grant-maintained. Francis Combe School is situated on the northern urban fringe of Watford, close to the M1 and the M25. Most of the children attending the school come from the council estates situated in this area. These estates are mostly within walking distance of the school although a substantial number of children travel by bus from north, central and west Watford. (The punctuality records of these pupils are at times influenced by an irregular service—unless they are prepared to arrive at school as early as 8 am.)

The late 1970s witnessed the construction of a new housing estate whose boundaries meet with those of the school. The close proximity of this estate, coupled with its 'rabbit warren'-like appearance has given those children intent on truanting the opportunity to do so with the knowledge that 'hiding places' are plentiful and close at hand. This and the other surrounding council estates are characterised by high unemployment and relatively high levels of social deprivation. It needs to be noted that many of the school's most supportive families live on these estates. One-third of the school's pupils receive free school meals.

Built in the early 1950s the school has enjoyed periods of mixed success, with the headship changing only four times during its 40 years. As one of the first comprehensives the school went through a period of great change in the 1960s. After a period of falling numbers and declining reputation, radical changes occurred in the middle 1970s with a considerable turnover in staff. A new clear ethos was established which focused on a 'whole school' approach, emphasising reward and praise for achievement and improvement. This centred on looking at the needs of each individual child, promoting success in whatever field and at whatever level was relevant and appropriate to that child. A strong pastoral system supported by an equally strong and committed team of teachers were encouraged by the findings of the Elton Report, the suggestions of which served to reinforce the positive work being done in the school. The school's reputation and popularity began to grow.

In the past three years extensive work has been undertaken in the area of secondary transfer and the school staff have continuously striven to raise the profile of the school in the eyes of the local community. The school has emerged with a reputation for caring deeply about both its pupils and its community and appears

ready and able to face the challenges of the future with optimism
and confidence.

Truancy—the formal picture

When the Project began at Francis Combe School we did not feel
that the school had a truancy problem. Indeed, the unauthorised
absence returns submitted to the DfE showed truancy levels of 1.2
per cent (percentage of sessions missed) and 16.9 per cent
(percentage of pupils with one or more unauthorised absence
against their names), scarcely, we felt, reason for great alarm. From
the beginning the Project was as concerned with promoting
attendance as with countering truancy. Having said this we had to
acknowledge that there were a few children who were having
difficulties, and surely one child experiencing attendance
difficulties is a reason for concern.

The official figures—the figures on which DfE unauthorised
absence returns are based—are, of course, derived from the
school's register. It can, however, be argued that some form
registers are notoriously unhelpful as tools in determining actual
levels of attendance. Different teachers within different schools,
regardless of their individual diligence as form tutors, tend to apply
their own criteria in determining whether an absence is authorised
or unauthorised. Form tutors are hard pressed and may not always
have the time or opportunity to follow up fully individual
incidences of absence. And in the context where they have to
publish levels of unauthorised absence in so-called truancy league
tables, schools may have a clear and obvious self-interest in
authorising as many absences as possible. Also registers, although
legal documents which schools are obliged to maintain and which
EWOs may use as evidence in court proceedings against the
parents of persistent non-attenders, do highlight just one form of
truancy—namely, blanket truancy (BT) (when the child is absent
without authorisation from the school). Registers take no account
whatsoever of post-registration truancy (PRT) (when the pupil
comes to school, registers and then proceeds to skip certain—
sometimes in extreme cases, all—lessons). In that it is not recorded
in the school register PRT has no legal status. Actual levels of PRT
are neither published nor indeed even known. It is astonishing that
so little research has been conducted into this phenomenon which
might just prove to be something of the hidden iceberg of non-
school attendance.

In spite of the fact that the register is universally recognised
as the school's main tool in determining its officially accepted

levels of attendance and the major means whereby those individual pupils who are experiencing attendance difficulties are identified, we felt that even the most excellently maintained register could contribute to create only a partial picture of the school's actual levels of truancy.

We wished to try and complete this picture and we believed that the most effective and useful way to do this would be to consult the pupils themselves. After all they were the ones who were doing the attending or the truanting, and it appeared unlikely that their responses would be coloured by the same considerations which might affect busy form tutors and anxious school managers. By consulting the pupils themselves we could also ask the truants what it was about school which was driving them to vote with their feet.

Accordingly, we decided to conduct a survey of the pupils at Francis Combe School in order to determine:

1. the nature and scale of truancy.
2. the reasons for truancy.
3. ways in which truancy could be reduced.

We also hoped to gain a few general pointers as to how Francis Combe School was regarded by all of its pupils—truants and non-truants alike.

The pupil survey

The pupil survey was carried out by means of an anonymous questionnaire. The only personal information which pupils were required to give was their gender and their year group. Ideally we would have liked to have consulted all those pupils of compulsory school age. The best time to have done this would have been the spring term. This would have enabled us to have elicited a meaningful response from Year 7 pupils who would by then have experienced one full term of secondary schooling and from Year 11 pupils all of whom would have then been in their last full term of compulsory schooling. The timing of the Project's funding, however, gave us little option other than to carry out our survey in the first few weeks of the summer term, thereby effectively disqualifying us from being able to consult systematically the Year 11 group, many of whom would have left the previous Easter. Had we waited until the autumn term we could have included the entire Year 11 group but this would have left us with no Year 7 pupils with any significant experience of secondary schooling. By the autumn term we would also have been halfway into our period of funding and we felt that our pupil survey—our 'patient consultation'—was a priority, an essential prerequisite to any diagnosis or course of treatment. Accordingly we settled on surveying Years 7, 8, 9, and 10. (The omission of Year 11, the year when, one assumes, truancy levels reach their highest, must mean that the survey findings give an under-representation of the real scale of truancy in the school—how much of an under-representation it is impossible to say accurately.)

The questionnaires were completed during form period time or during PSE lessons in a setting which was informal yet ordered. Pupils filled in the questionnaires on their own, without consulting with their friends. They were assured of the anonymity of their responses and were invited and positively encouraged to be as open and as honest as they wished. It was stressed that the questionnaire was in no way part of a 'checking-up' exercise.

It could be argued that most of the truants would have been truanting when the questionnaires were completed and that therefore the body of truants would not have been represented in the survey findings. In fact, on the days when the questionnaires were completed very few pupils were actually absent and those who were completed their questionnaires on their return. Total anonymity was assured and maintained throughout.

Of course, pupils sitting in a school classroom, surrounded by their school friends, supervised by a teacher, being asked to fill in a questionnaire on school attendance may not surprisingly have had school-related factors at the forefront of their minds as they reflected on how they were to answer some questions—most notably those questions seeking the motivation for acts of truancy. While it was clearly important to keep this in mind in assessing the results of the survey we did not feel that it in any way undermined or invalidated the conclusions that we could draw. The purpose of our survey was to assist us not only in gaining a complete picture of levels and patterns of unauthorised absence but also to help us to develop ways of encouraging more pupils to attend school regularly. The survey had to be much more than a piece of research. Its findings had to inform and guide our future practice. In this respect we were purposefully seeking to locate those school-related factors which discouraged some pupils from attending. Of course, we recognised that other factors—home circumstances, the individual pupil's psychology, etc., all affect school attendance, but it is only over school-related factors that schools can exercise some meaningful and effective control. Accordingly, we envisaged the survey primarily as a guide to action.

Neither Project worker was a trained researcher and this was the first time that either of us had engaged in such a piece of work. Not surprisingly a few mistakes were made. We have already mentioned our concerns over the timing of the survey—but here we were very much the prisoners of factors outside of our control.

There were, however, difficulties that we might have foreseen—
easily said with the benefit of hindsight! Some of the questions
appear, in retrospect, either clumsily or naively worded. Some—
albeit a minority—of the data were of dubious value. (Masses of
data are only of some worth if they serve some purpose!)
Frustratingly we neglected to ask certain key questions—most
notably, we failed to ask non-truants why it was that they didn't
truant, or more constructively why it was that they regularly
attended. Ideally, it would have been useful to have undertaken a
small pilot survey with a selected group of pupils, gone away and
engaged in a period of critical reflection, and then returned with a
modified and refined questionnaire. But, to repeat, time dictated
our schedule. (When a follow-up survey is conducted we will
certainly avoid the pitfalls and shortcomings of the first.)

Essentially, however, we were delighted with the response to,
and the outcome of, the survey. The vast majority of pupils—
probably all—appeared to enjoy being consulted about how *they*
felt about *their* school. At the end of the questionnaire pupils were
asked to add any comments about school or school attendance.
Surprisingly—or maybe we should not be surprised—not one pupil
among the 339 who completed questionnaires felt the need or the
desire to make an offensive or destructive comment. Here was an
ideal opportunity, in the safety of guaranteed anonymity, to off-
load any pent-up emotion or hostility. In fact, all the comments
made were polite, well-intentioned and in most cases very sensible
and eminently practical.

The survey findings

Main points

- Truancy, both BT and PRT, does not exist on any significant
  scale in Years 7 and 8, although it does begin to become more
  pronounced in Years 9 and 10.
- BT increases steadily between Years 7 and 10. PRT, however,
  increases considerably more steeply after Year 8 (although
  surprisingly it fell slightly in Year 10).
- The mean BT figure for the school (i.e. those pupils who
  engaged in one or more acts of BT in the past year) is 20.4 per
  cent.
- The mean PRT figure for the school (i.e. those pupils who have
  engaged in one or more acts of PRT in the past year) is 30.4 per
  cent.
- The mean figure for those pupils who have engaged in both BT
  and PRT in the past year is 15.6 per cent.

- The majority of truants (both BT and PRT) claim to engage in truancy 'hardly ever' (i.e. once a half-term).
- The hard core of truants—those who claim to truant 'frequently' (i.e. more than three times a half-term) represent a very small minority of the pupil population.
- Parentally condoned truancy, while being extremely difficult to locate with any precision, does not appear to exist on any significant scale.
- The major reason given why pupils truant is that they experience particular difficulties with particular lessons or with particular teachers. This applies both to BT and to PRT, but especially to the latter.
- Truanting appears to be a social activity in which pupils engage with their friends. There is, however, no evidence to suggest that peer pressure influences pupils to truant.
- There is no evidence of any widespread disaffection with school. On the contrary, most pupils appear to have a positive attitude towards school. Only 17 pupils (five per cent) said that they disliked school.
- The future intentions of most pupils appear to be very positive. Only 22 pupils (6.5 per cent) said that they would 'probably' truant in the future.

The scale and nature of truancy

Extent of blanket truancy

Table 4.1 Pupils admitting to one or more acts of BT in the past year

Year	Total pupils	Blanket truants	%
7	70	5	7.1
8	83	10	12
9	75	19	25.3
10	111	35	31.5
	339	69	20.4

Extent of post-registration truancy

Table 4.2 Pupils admitting to one or more acts of PRT in the past year

Year	Total pupils	Post-registration truants	%
7	70	5	7.1
8	83	13	15.7
9	75	37	49.3
10	111	48	43.2
	339	103	30.4

The BT figures, while no reason for complacency, were very much as we might have anticipated. What did surprise us and set us thinking, however, were the PRT levels, especially those for Years 9 and 10.

Extent of blanket and post-registration truancy

Table 4.3   Pupils admitting to engaging in both BT and PRT in the past year

Year	Total pupils	Blanket truants and post-registration truants	%
7	70	2	2.9
8	83	6	7.2
9	75	16	21.3
10	111	29	26.1
	339	53	15.6

Frequency of truancy

In looking at the frequency of truancy we used the following classifications:

- 'Hardly ever'—once a half-term.
- 'Sometimes'—two or three times a half-term.
- 'Frequently'—more than three times a half-term.

Table 4.4   Frequency of BT

Year	7	8	9	10	Total	%
Hardly ever	5	6	14	19	44	63.8
Sometimes	0	3	4	10	17	24.6
Frequently	0	1	1	6	8	11.6
Total	5	10	19	35	69	

Table 4.5   Frequency of PRT

Year	7	8	9	10	Total	%
Hardly ever	4	9	23	31	67	65.1
Sometimes	0	2	12	9	23	22.3
Frequently	1	2	2	8	13	12.6
Total	5	13	37	48	103	

Extent of parentally condoned truancy

This category of truancy is notoriously difficult to identify with any precision. Our findings here were of limited value but what we did discover was that around 40 per cent of parents knew of their child's truancy. Of these the overwhelming majority responded with either 'anger' or 'worry'. Only one pupil in the entire school suggested that his/her parents were unconcerned by his/her truancy.

Reasons offered to explain truancy

Blanket truancy

Table 4.6   Reasons offered to explain BT

Reasons offered	Year	7	8	9	10	Total	%
1. Disaffection with school		2	4	2	6	14	20.3
2. Lesson difficulty		1	5	14	20	40	58
3. Peer pressure		1	0	0	2	3	4.3
4. Bullying		0	0	0	0	0	0
5. Other		1	1	3	7	12	17.4
		5	10	19	35	69	

Table 4.7   Reasons offered to explain PRT

Reasons offered	Year	7	8	9	10	Total	%
1. Disaffection with school		0	1	0	1	2	1.9
2. Lesson difficulty		2	7	30	32	71	69
3. Peer pressure		0	0	1	1	2	1.9
4. Bullying		0	0	1	0	1	1
5. Other		3	5	5	14	27	26.2
		5	13	37	48	103	

In the questionnaire pupils who admitted to an act of truancy were then asked to write a few words explaining their reasons. Not everyone did this. Those who did were separated into five general categories. 'Bullying', 'Peer pressure' and 'Dissaffection with school' are self-explanatory. 'Other' covered such comments as 'I don't know', 'Because I felt like it', etc. Under 'Lesson difficulty' we included such comments as 'The lessons are boring', 'I didn't want to go to maths', 'The lessons are too hard', 'Because I have a subject teacher I don't like', 'Because I'm not good at that lesson and I look stupid', etc.

While we were surprised that not one pupil cited bullying as a reason for BT and only one pupil cited it as a reason for PRT we were intrigued by the numbers who advanced lesson difficulty as the motivating factor behind their act(s) of truancy. Words and phrases such as 'boring', 'hard', 'don't like' and 'can't do' cropped up time and time again. A few pupils mentioned the specific subjects which they felt the most antipathy towards. Maths, French and PE appeared to be the most unpopular.

Clearly there were some areas of the curricular and pedagogic process which a small but significant number of pupils were rejecting. School itself was not the problem.

Nor was the general process of learning. Rather it appeared that certain aspects of the curriculum were found by some pupils to be either inaccessible, inappropriate, irrelevant or simply boring. Those pupils who were truanting were clearly making a rational choice when confronted by the curriculum menu which was being offered to them. Of course, we need to remember that the vast majority of pupils go to the vast majority of lessons. Lesson dissatisfaction as a reason for truancy must be kept within this context.

Other findings

Ease of truancy

A total of 60.9 per cent of pupils who had truanted (BT) said that their parents were unaware of their truancy. Some 50.7 per cent said that their teachers were unaware. This would suggest that blanket truants have a more than even chance of avoiding detection.

PRT appears only slightly more risky: 47.6 per cent of post-registration truants said that they had done so undetected.

Sociability of truancy

Some 68.7 per cent of truants (both BT and PRT) said that when they truanted they did so in the company of their friends. At the end of the questionnaire several non-truants commented that they enjoyed school because it meant being with their friends. Clearly the acceptance or rejection of aspects of school has a considerable social dimension.

Popularity of school

One of the most encouraging findings from the survey was the total lack of any widespread antipathy towards or alienation from school. Not only did this emerge in the number of favourable comments offered at the end of the questionnaire but more directly in answers to the question, 'Do you like school?'—as shown in Table 4.8.

Table 4.8 Popularity of school

Year	7	8	9	10	Total	%
Yes	40	31	21	49	141	41.6
No	1	5	7	4	17	5
Sometimes	29	47	47	58	181	53.4
	70	83	75	111	339	

Where truants go and what they do

When confronted by questions of where they went and what they did most truants took advantage of the covering advice, 'You do not have to answer this question'. Perhaps, especially in the case of PRT, it was somewhat naive to have expected truants to reveal their sanctuaries and their activities. There were, however, some replies. In response to the question 'Where do you go?' most of these replies were along the lines of 'To the shops', 'To a mate's house', 'In the toilets', 'Nowhere in particular'. Responses to the question 'What do you do?' were along similar lines—'Just hang around', 'Nothing much', 'Sit and chat', 'Wait for the bell to go'! Such answers would suggest that truancy can have a casual sociability about it.

General

The survey did suggest that girls are more ready than boys to engage in truancy (both BT and PRT) but the difference was marginal and we felt unable to draw any firm conclusions from this. The future intentions of most pupils regarding their attendance appear to be positive. Only 22 (6.5 per cent) said that they would 'probably' truant in the future. Of the remainder 73 (21.5 per cent) said that 'perhaps' they would truant, while 244 (72 per cent) said that they were 'unlikely' to. This provided us with considerable grounds for optimism. Clearly we had to support the 244, encourage the 73, and dissuade the 22.

Pupils' comments

As we have remarked, at the end of the questionnaire pupils were invited to add any comments which they might like to make on school or school attendance. Most pupils took advantage of this and we were presented with a wealth of comments, advice and suggestions. We grouped these under four general headings and offer below a selection from each:

1. **Reasons offered for regular attendance**
   'Our school is brilliant and I love it.' 'I like school. I don't think it's worth bunking because your lesson is only for an hour and if you don't like it it's tough.' 'It's a good school because they reward you for being good.' 'Not many people truant so we must be doing something right.'
2. **Fears and criticisms**
   'I wouldn't skip as much if lessons were a bit more interesting.' 'I only bunked once because the teacher was being unfair to

me.' 'School gets tiring.' 'Some people skip because they are worried about school.'

3. **Suggestions for changes in school practice**
   'The registration system should change to make it more difficult for children to truant.' 'Teachers should be more strict.' 'Lessons and school should be made more interesting.' 'Truants should be encouraged to come back to school but they should not be bribed.' 'I think the school should be cleaned up and redecorated.'

4. **General comments**
   'I think it's bad missing school and I regret it.' 'I only truant to take a break and I don't do it all the time.' 'I don't like school but I don't really play truant because if I get caught I'm in big trouble at home.' 'Attendance is better than at most schools but we have people who come to be registered and then go home.' 'I hope that there will not be league tables produced on these surveys. I believe league tables are a stupid idea.' 'When I miss a lesson I do it on my own. I've only done it twice in four years—surely no harm can come of that.' 'I don't like the way that some teachers know that pupils are missing but don't do anything about it—I know that teachers are thankful to get some kids out of their lessons.' 'The last time I skipped a lesson was ages ago and I'm past bunking now because school is far too important and I enjoy it now (most of the time).'

All of these comments were fascinating and while one or two made us feel slightly uncomfortable we certainly had to sit up and take note. We had asked pupils for their frank comments; they had given them. The challenge for us was to respond constructively.

Conclusion

The manner in which we responded to the survey would, in large measure, be a barometer of how useful it had been. As we have emphasised, the survey was intended to highlight those areas of the school experience which needed to be further explored, developed and improved. This process has begun in a number of areas.

- The school is actively striving to develop and improve the curricular and pedagogic experience which pupils receive. It is easy to say that schools should deliver a lively, relevant and accessible curriculum. The challenge is how to achieve this in practice.
- The school's Special Needs Department is exploring new ways of responding to the needs of those pupils who experience difficulty in accessing the curriculum.

- Support mechanisms for teachers who have to deal with particularly disruptive pupils are being developed.
- Strategies for countering PRT are being constantly monitored and reviewed (all staff are requested to carry out register checks for each lesson, out-of-lesson slips have been introduced, spot-checks are made, etc.).
- Attendance and punctuality have been given a high profile throughout the school. Regular attendance reports are carried in school bulletins, newsletters, etc. The importance of good attendance is highlighted by means of a display board in the school foyer featuring photographs of all those pupils who achieve 100 per cent attendance over the school year and a large graph featuring the school's overall weekly attendance level.
- Issues of attendance/punctuality have been incorporated into a whole-school curricular pastoral merit system. Achievement is acknowledged and rewarded. The importance of improvement—however small—is constantly stressed.
- All staff—not just form tutors and year heads—are being asked to share in responsibility for attendance matters.
- Recording systems are being constantly reviewed. While the form register is still used as the major tool for identifying those pupils who may be experiencing attendance difficulties it is never used in isolation.
- The school's partnership with its EWO has been further developed and consultation visits are now much more focused.
- Major refurbishments are underway to improve the sociability/conviviality of the school. (Funds for much of this work are being sought by the headteacher from a multiplicity of extra-school and extra-LEA sources.)
- Clear school policies on attendance and punctuality are being introduced and communicated to pupils, and parents.

We believe good levels of school attendance to be important not because of published league tables—such tables appear to be of dubious value—but because good attendance is important in its own right, as an essential prerequisite to effective learning. At Francis Combe School we are constantly striving to improve our levels of attendance. Before a school can begin to look at how it may achieve any improvement, however, it must have a view and understanding of how things stand at that moment. Our pupil survey helped us towards achieving such a view and understanding. It is an exercise which we shall certainly repeat in the future.

We would strongly recommend that other schools carry out their own pupil surveys. The results can give a reasonably clear picture of actual levels and patterns of attendance and can provide the school with a useful tool with which to identify those areas of school life which may need to be further explored and developed. A pupil survey can give the stakeholders in the school an opportunity to openly and honestly express their views on what makes school an attractive or an unattractive experience. It can encourage a school to be frank and direct with itself. And—very importantly—it can be fun.

Part II
Managing
the problem

5 Policies for improving attendance

Patricia Stoll

Introduction

The findings of the report *Truancy in English Secondary Schools* (O'Keeffe, 1994) provide a strong base for formulating policies for improving attendance and curbing truancy. Most pupils in the sample said that they liked school and thought that most of what they are learning will be useful to them in the future. Although a disturbing number of the pupils said that they had truanted in the previous six weeks (30.5 per cent) the majority had not done so. The reasons these pupils gave are extremely useful when considering ways of improving attendance and they are analysed below.

There is, however, no easy solution to the problem of truancy and poor attendance. Dealing with truancy is rather like seeking a cure for a disease. First a correct diagnosis has to be made if the appropriate treatment is to be administered. Nor does the same medicine necessarily suit every person, as in the case of, for example, antibiotics. So it is with truancy. Schools must first of all diagnose the problem before defining ways of dealing with it. Teachers need to understand the truancy phenomenon and its various manifestations. This is what the O'Keeffe report set out to do.

Truancy: BT and PRT

It is important for those members of staff who have special responsibility for improving attendance in their establishments to identify the *type* and *level* of truancy in their particular school. For example, the report indicates that the problem of blanket truancy (BT) is greater in inner-city schools. A school which does not have very much BT may have a problem with post-registration truancy (PRT). The reason is that if a pupil's blanket truancy is detected and the boy or girl is forced back into school, he or she may truant from a lesson or lessons that are particularly unpalatable.

Ideally, some form of truancy mapping should take place before policies are made. The school would then know what kind of truancy is occurring and the frequency of the truancy. Teachers would be in a strong position to act upon this information. Too many schools think that if the registers show a marked improvement in attendance they have addressed the problem. But if staff put all their energies into concentrating on dealing with BT and ignore PRT then they have not necessarily dealt with truancy in their school.

Truancy: a problem in all schools

We visited 150 schools in our survey and administered confidential questionnaires to all pupils in Years 10 and 11 who were present on the day of the survey. Not a single school had no truancy whatsoever. The lowest level was 13 per cent and the highest was 50 per cent. The average was about 22 per cent. Truancy may not be a big problem in some schools but we think it highly unlikely that there is no truancy at all in any school. During our research study we became aware that many schools underestimate the extent of truancy and indeed seem to be unaware of truancy, particularly post-registration, mainly because it is so much more difficult to identify.

The scale of truancy

The findings of the report are undeniably worrying and, because of the size of the sample, we believe them not to be atypical. A significant minority of pupils in Years 10 and 11 admitted to truanting at least once in the previous six weeks. If the time scale had been larger we have reason to believe that the number of pupils saying they had truanted would have been much higher.[1] Few of the truants said that they truanted from school only (10.3 per cent) and only just over a quarter (25.2 per cent) said that they truanted from lessons only. The vast majority of truants (64.4 per cent) said that they sometimes truanted from school and sometimes from lessons and within the subset, more pupils truanted from lessons than from school.

Pupil attitudes to school

Despite such widespread truancy the majority of pupils in the survey—including truants—said that they like school most of the time. Almost half of the non-truants and nearly a third of the truants said that school is 'mostly enjoyable'. The number of truants who said that they liked school is surprisingly high and suggests that there is no deep alienation or widespread disaffection on the part of pupils. It is also worth noting that very few pupils— 4 per cent of non-truants and 17 per cent of truants—said that they never find school enjoyable. School is, after all, a place where young people meet and socialise with their friends. Indeed, it is this aspect of school life that is very important when looking at ways of improving attendance.

Both the truants and the non-truants in the survey said that they regarded *most* of what they are learning in school now as useful to them when they leave school. As many as 77 per cent of non-truants and 65 per cent of truants said that half to most of what they are learning is useful. Very few—one per cent of non-truants and six per cent of truants—said that none of what they are learning is useful.

Possibly the most encouraging statistic of all is the response the pupils gave when asked if they wished to continue their education after Year 11. Unsurprisingly 75 per cent of non-truants want to continue but as many as 58 per cent of truants and 66 per cent of post-registration truants want to continue.

There is much evidence then that the majority of pupils like school and value their learning despite a large number of truants (20 per cent) giving dislike of lessons as the only reason for truanting. It is not all lessons but only parts of the curricular fare that are being rejected.

Why non-truants do not truant

The report has much to tell us which can help when considering ways of improving attendance and combating truancy. First, what is important here is the information given by the pupils who do not truant. There are three main reasons given for not truanting.

Almost half (48 per cent) of non-truants said that they did not do so because their parents might find out, 40 per cent said that they did not want to miss school and almost the same number said that their teachers might find out. Pupils could give more than one answer if they so wished. As we have said in the report, the data are consistent—and no more than this is claimed—with schools being popular socially rather than intellectually. The fact that 40 per cent said that they did not want to miss school could subsume approval of the curriculum.

Schools with the lowest levels of truancy

What can be learned from the schools in our survey which had the lowest levels of truancy? We compared the 25 schools with the lowest levels of truancy and the 25 schools with the highest levels. Not surprisingly, the 25 schools with the largest percentages of truants finding truancy easy had the highest truancy levels (34 per cent) and the 25 schools with the smallest percentages of truants finding truancy easy had the lowest levels (26 per cent). We made similar comparisons with schools using as the base non-truants deterred from truancy by the possibility of the school finding out. In the 25 schools with the highest number of such non-truants the truancy levels were lowest (26 per cent) and highest (36 per cent) in the 25 schools with the lowest number of non-truants deterred by the possibility of the school finding out.

Clearly, school ethos plays a major role in combating truancy and promoting good attendance. Below are two school models which outline practical measures for improving attendance.

School-based policies for improving attendance and combating truancy

One north London comprehensive school, which shall be named School A for purposes of confidentiality, has developed successful strategies for improving attendance over a three-year period. The project came about as a result of the Elton report *Discipline in Schools* which was published by the then Department of Education and Science (DES) in 1989. The government decided to award local education authorities (LEAs) grants to improve attendance in schools. These grants were known as ESG—education support grant—and were the forerunner of the present GEST—grants for education support and training. LEAs were invited to bid for ESG for a three-year period. School A's authority decided to focus on one secondary school—School A—and four of its feeder primary schools. The emphasis was on *improving* attendance.

When the project began in 1990 School A had 720 pupils aged 11 to 18 years. It was undersubscribed and had an overall attendance rate of 72 per cent during the academic year before the project began. There were a large number of casual admissions and this situation has continued. In the academic year 1992/3, for example, there were 115 admissions and 40 pupils left. Forty-three community languages are represented. The school was selected by the LEA because of poor attendance records and feedback from the Education Welfare Service (EWS). It was not unusual for the school Education Welfare Officer (EWO) to receive as many as 40 referrals in a week. The authority decided to concentrate resources in this one particular school and make the project entirely school-based. It was imperative, therefore, to have a key person in the school, someone with a high profile of leadership. A senior teacher and member of the senior management team was appointed to set up the project and bring about the necessary changes.

The target set was a 15 per cent overall improvement in attendance. This was a purely arbitrary figure and was considered by the HMI involved in the project to be unrealistic. However, by the end of the first year the attendance rate had risen to 77 per cent, by the end of the second year to 85 per cent and the target figure of 90 per cent was achieved in the final year of the project.

Under ESG funding there was money available for capital expenditure. This was spent on 'social bases' which were rooms allocated to Year groups where pupils could come and socialise, a computer and an additional EWO. A .5 educational psychologist was appointed as well as a .6 supply teacher per primary school. There was also a SMSA—school midday supervisory assistant—and an administration assistant appointed.

A steering committee comprising the five headteachers of the schools, inspectors and the project team was set up to monitor the project. They met once a term. The members of the project management group decided to concentrate initially on the implication of nine strategies. They were: making the school a welcoming place, information, incentives, curriculum, registers, staff, the EWS, primary links and practice and, finally, dissemination. Each is worthy of consideration.

Making school a welcoming place

The project team began by putting their efforts into making their school a welcoming place. A special room was set aside for visitors. It was equipped with comfortable chairs and toys for young children; samples of pupils' work decorated the walls. Twelve thousand pounds was allocated to the setting up of the social bases. Pupils in Years 7 and 8 shared one large area and Years 9, 10 and 11 pupils were given a room per Year group. The rooms contained chairs, coffee tables, television sets and video recorders. The bases were set up because previously pupils were never allowed on to the school premises in the morning, during breaks, at lunch times and after school. When the social bases started the pupils themselves drew up a contract and they supervised the rooms themselves.

The high number of casual admissions was a problem. As part of the initiative to make the school a welcoming place, form tutors, with the ESL (English as a Second Language) department devised a 'Welcome' pack. This was designed and put together by pupils during Personal, Social and Health Education (PSHE) time. It comprised a timetable, teachers' names and profiles, pupils' profiles, lesson times and a green card which stated 'If I look lost ...'. Each class in the school produced three copies. This was so successful in integrating new pupils into the school that a similar approach was introduced when a non-attender was brought back to school by the EWO.

Information

The publishing of information was important for the success of the project. The project leader was present at all senior management meetings and consequently was able to push through the changes. He also attended governors' meetings and updated the board of governors on the progress of the project. Weekly bulletins concerning attendance were produced and attendance league tables were exhibited. Newsletters were sent regularly to schools in the LEA. Each week the project team considered every child whose attendance was below 80 per cent. Targets were set to help each child to improve his or her attendance. During assemblies attendance was rewarded. Separate meetings for Key Stage 3 (KS3) and Key Stage 4 (KS4) were held every Monday morning. The school discovered that Monday training days for staff badly affected attendance for the rest of the week. Activities Week, which was held four weeks before the end of the summer term, was regarded by many pupils as the start of the long summer holidays. This event is now held during the penultimate week of the school year. School examination week on the other hand has an excellent effect on attendance.

Incentives

A number of rewards for good attendance were awarded. They included: pens inscribed with the school's name for 100 per cent attendance in any one term, key-rings with coin holders for 100 per cent attendance in two terms and a mug and photograph for 100 per cent attendance in the whole school year. In the first year of the project only nine pupils were awarded mugs but in the second year 51 pupils won this award. This illustrates the trend. The reward system includes keyrings for improvers. An added incentive is the use of coloured stickers in homework diaries including a gold one for one week's full attendance.

Curriculum

During PSHE time form tutors and staff worked together. Every teaching period was double-staffed. The teachers concerned might team teach or one might spend the time completing records of achievement while the other teacher teaches the group. They might use the time to talk to poor attenders and set targets. Part-time timetables were devised for long-term absentees returning to school. This was to ensure that attendance did not break down the minute a pupil returned to the classroom.

The major innovation was the introduction of three-year GCSEs. As a result of so many pupils not being able to cope with seven or eight GCSEs many pupils now go into the Sixth Form and take their examinations at the end of Year 12. This has, of course, imposed restrictions on timetabling because the teachers who were teaching Year 11 courses have to be timetabled to continue the teaching of these courses in Year 12.

Registers

In any attempt to improve attendance the first priority is to ensure that the school registers are accurate. The project team developed the authority's Project Codes for the front of the registers. These have now been superseded by the official Department for Education (DfE) regulations which came into force in 1992. The marking of the registers was standardised in School A and the project primary schools as well. A way of collating 'Unauthorised/ authorised absence' running totals was piloted in Year 8 during the final year of the project.

Staff

It is important to stress that the project was a whole school project. If it had not been it is doubtful whether it would have been so successful. The project staff and the school staff worked as a team. The EWO and the Educational Psychologist were known to all the pupils and both had a high profile in the school. Each Head of Year had a senior teacher attached to the Year. Senior teachers and other senior staff were all form tutors.

The Education Welfare Service

The EWS had a very big role to play in the project. Initially there were two, one from the EWS and one financed by the project. The EWO always attended the weekly KS3 and KS4 meetings. He also attended PSHE lessons regularly and went into other lessons to help pupils, particularly those who had been absent for a long time and needed support in their reintegration into school.

Primary school links

Links with the primary schools were developed and strengthened during the course of the project. A special room was allocated for the use of visiting primary school staff and pupils. A project staff member visited the primary schools on a regular basis with the EWO. The purpose was to prepare Year 6 pupils for their week's visit to School A as part of their preparation for transfer to secondary school.

Dissemination

Part of the project staff's brief was that the school should be able to share with the other schools in the authority what they had developed at School A. Consequently the project staff held a two-day INSET programme on attendance in October 1990. They have provided training for all their LEA's primary staff and for all secondary schools and EWOs. They have given regular presentations on the 'Attendance and Truancy' courses organised by the Truancy Unit at the University of North London.

At the time that the project was set up the school had a bad reputation. There were fights, drugs, Union action, and so on. This reputation was very hard to combat but most of these problems have now been overcome. The atmosphere in the school has improved during the course of the project and, perhaps most telling of all, staff absenteeism has been greatly reduced. The school is firmly convinced that all this has come about by putting in place the nine strategies outlined here. To achieve this it was necessary to adopt a four-fold approach:

1. The staff were positive about attendance and worked primarily with those pupils who were in school. They had been advised by inspectors not to concentrate initially on 'school refusers' but rather on intermittent attenders. Achievement of any kind had not been hitherto recognised. That situation has been completely changed.
2. The project team concentrated on preventive work. An important part of this work was done by the EWO when attending lesson and working with pupils.
3. Targets were set for pupils and when they were met the pupils were rewarded.
4. The team concentrated on making school a welcoming place.

To sum up, the school promoted positive attitudes among the members of staff, which were then reflected in the ethos and culture of the school. Leadership, co-operation, parental involvement, a system of rewards and punishments—all were necessary for improving attendance. It should not be overlooked, however, that the school received substantial funding to run the project. It is possible nevertheless to undertake measures to improve attendance without having to spend large sums of money. A second school model—the school shall be named School B again for purposes of confidentiality—achieved a notable improvement in attendance and diminished truancy considerably without significant expenditure.

School B is a large, popular voluntary-aided mixed comprehensive school in south London. It is not dissimilar to School A in many respects as its intake is comparable and it has its fair share of casual admissions. It is, however, more popular than School A, which may largely be due to its Church affiliation. School B suffered from poor attendance and high truancy rates until a few years ago when a new headteacher was appointed to the school. He was dismayed by the high rate of truancy in the school and decided to give this matter top priority. It was decided that the problem would be tackled in three ways:

1. Discipline in general would be tightened.
2. The security of the buildings would be looked at with a view to closing all bolt-holes.
3. The curriculum would be scrutinised and particular consideration would be given to addressing the needs of the less able pupils.

Discipline

All pupils were issued with Day Books in which they were to enter their homework. The books were used as a means of monitoring the pupil's progress and whereabouts during the course of the day. If a child leaves a classroom during lesson time he or she must have a note written by the teacher in the Day Book.

The detention system was tightened up. There was a hierarchical order—subject teacher's detention, faculty detention, Year and head's detention. This final detention, the most serious of all, was of one hour's duration and given only for severe misdemeanours and to those pupils who were persistent offenders. A letter would be sent home to parents informing them of the child's detention and emphasising the seriousness of the offence. Truants given the head's detention would spend their time making up the work that they had missed as a result of their truancy. Persistent truants are put on report and the parents are interviewed by the child's head of year. A letter is sent to the parent of a child who has been absent for two days and this letter is then followed up by a telephone call. The heads of year are timetabled to meet the school's Education Social Worker once a week.

A head of upper school and one of lower school were appointed specifically to deal with matters of discipline. The number of lessons in the school day was reduced from eight periods to six, four in the morning and two in the afternoon, as an attempt to reduce movement around the school and lessen opportunities for truanting. The lunch hour was reduced by fifteen minutes and the school day ended at ten minutes past three. Toilets and locker rooms were locked during lesson time and special permission would have to be sought from a teacher to visit the toilets during lessons. This arrangement is controversial and would be unacceptable to many teachers. As a temporary measure, however, it might be justified.

Security

Teachers were asked to be vigilant at all times and be prepared to challenge children who were out of class. Previously, some teachers—particularly the least experienced—had been reluctant to ask children why they were out of class. This was mainly because of lack of confidence on the part of teachers who did not wish to find themselves in situations with which they might not be able to cope. With strong support from senior teachers with responsibility for discipline—there is a deputy head based in every Year block as well as the head of year—that situation has now changed. In addition, frequent 'spot' checks are made on attendance during lesson time. Pupils are aware, therefore, that attempts at post-registration truancy are likely to be detected.

It was agreed that disruptive children would not be put out of classrooms. A child who misbehaves is sent to the relevant faculty or year head with work to do.

As well as the locking during lesson time of such apparent bolt-holes as toilets and lockers, the front and back exit gates are monitored by security cameras. This surveillance system was installed initially after an attack on a schoolkeeper by an intruder. One of the spin-offs has been the facility to expose the unauthorised departure from the building by truants. There have been cases where pupils were identified and the parents informed immediately. By the time the child reached home the parent already knew that he or she was truanting from school. Our truancy report showed that pupils are deterred from truancy if they know that their parents and the school will find out.

School B has not only taken Draconian measures to deal with truancy. The staff believed, just as the teachers at School A did, that it was important to make the school a welcoming place, a place where pupils and teachers want to be. The school arranged for an ice-cream van to come on site during the lunch hour in the summer term. A school tuck shop was provided to deter pupils from wanting to go out during breaks or the lunch hour. A breakfast bar serving hot food has proved to be very popular. This facility has encouraged punctuality as well as providing breakfast for many children who would otherwise go without.

Curriculum

The school was aware of the part the curriculum has to play in truancy among pupils. Senior members of staff decided to look for examinations that were suitable for failing candidates. A Life Skills course was set up in Years 10 and 11 for those pupils who were struggling with the mainstream curriculum. It did not prevent them from taking GCSEs but rather prepared pupils, who might otherwise not have been able to take any examinations, to take some.

Truants with emotional problems were given a short-term 'sheltered' education in the Special Needs department. A Girls' Group was set up by the head of the department to help teenage girls with matters of diet, dress, etc. The purpose of these lunch-time sessions was to help girls improve their self-confidence.

The school was aware of the particular part that games and PE play in the problem of truancy. Our research has shown this to be the case.[2] The PE department investigated the possibility of offering aerobics and 'keep fit' classes to reluctant students of PE. Unfortunately a teacher needs special qualifications to teach such classes, which most trained teachers do not have at present.

As a result of carrying out these measures there has been a marked improvement in pupils' punctuality, there has been much less blanket truancy and there is now very little PRT. There is an atmosphere of calm and order. Pupils know where they stand and are aware of the consequences if they step out of line. School B is an oversubscribed school. It is popular with parents because of its high standard of discipline and behaviour which is reflected in good attendance and very little truancy.

The findings of the report and the achievements of Schools A and B show that there is a great deal that schools can do to improve attendance. It is much more difficult to deal with PRT than BT. A blanket truant's absence is known to the school because he or she is marked absent in the class register. Post-registration truants on the other hand are attending school. They have registered in the morning and the afternoon and then absented themselves from one or more lessons. Teachers need to be punctilious about keeping lesson registers and heads of year might find it worthwhile to carry out regular 'spot' checks. Both these measures will go a long way to combat PRT—as long as the information received is acted upon. We have shown that in schools where pupils truant with impunity the levels of truancy are high. Schools need to have in place policies for dealing with both BT and PRT. You cannot expect to cure the problem but you may at least be able to reduce truancy to a level that is no longer serious.

Notes

1. In our previous study—Stoll, P. and O'Keeffe, D.J. (1989) *Officially Present; An investigation into post-registration truancy in nine maintained schools*, London: IEA Education Unit—pupils in their final year of school were asked if they had truanted at least once since beginning their GCSE courses five terms previously. Two-thirds of the pupils said that they had.
2. We found this to be so not only in the two studies already cited but also in Stoll, P. 'Post-Registration Truancy: A Study', thesis submitted to the Polytechnic of North London for Master of Philosophy degree in October 1989.

References

O'Keeffe, D.J. (1994) *Truancy in English Secondary Schools*, London, HMSO.

6 Rethinking the image of the truant

Colin Coldman

Introduction

Truancy is against the law. The widespread knowledge that this is so may explain why the popular image of the truant, as social deviant and young offender, is firmly fixed in the public consciousness. It is less often noted that it is the parent of the truant who is the law-breaker (even if the parent is unaware of the truancy). It is easy to see, however, how this criminal image of truancy is established. If the truant is seen as going against the law in the act of truancy itself, and is also viewed as inevitably being up to no good when absent from school, then the link to petty, and not so petty, crime is a natural one. This is one widespread image of truancy and one that is generally unhelpful even though it contains elements of truth. It is unhelpful mainly because it concentrates on one particular activity that some truants indulge in but cannot explain truancy as a social phenomenon or help us understand it. Indeed, the link between truancy and teenage crime is likely to be of more interest to someone studying youth crime than truancy. It is particularly unfortunate, therefore, that this minor adjunct to the truancy debate has come to be central to government thinking on the issue.

Another image of the truant is the deficiency model, where the child is seen as truanting because of some personal inadequacy or social problem. The truant is seen as 'disaffected', which of course he may be, but it is assumed that this is irrational behaviour on the part of the truant because, in absenting himself from school, he is excluding himself from education (which is desired by rational people). This view of truancy is more prominent within education theory and practice. As with the previous image of truancy, this view has its merits and can be used with limited success. The problem of both models, however, is that they can generate only strictly limited theories of truancy which ignore both the scope and the pattern of truancy as a social phenomenon. Both models tend to a view of truancy as a marginal and separate problem for schools to counter. Perhaps this view is one akin to bullying—worrying where it occurs but not centrally important to the way the curriculum is determined or implemented.

The third model of truancy is the one proposed by the work of O'Keeffe and Stoll (1994), where the truant is seen as acting rationally. It is this image that constitutes the best explanatory model for the statistical evidence that truancy is both widespread and not restricted to certain groups of pupils or areas of the country. This is not to say that this model is comprehensive. Clearly some truants *are* involved in crime and many truant because of social problems. No doubt some truants are inadequates. The O'Keeffe/Stoll model, however, gives far more potential for developing a useful heuristic for the study of widespread truancy. It also has the epistemological merit of not denying the truths contained in other models of truancy.

Below is an outline of some of the key statistical evidence gathered by the University of North London Truancy Unit, which it is argued cannot be explained by the criminal or deficiency images of truancy. Unless otherwise stated, all the statistics on truancy used in this chapter are taken from *Truancy in English Secondary Schools* (O'Keeffe, 1994).

The size and scope of the problem

Financed by the Department for Education, the University of North London Truancy Unit conducted a survey by confidential questionnaire of 37,683 pupils in 150 schools chosen randomly from the state secondary schools of England. All the pupils surveyed were in Year 10 or 11. This is by far the largest empirical study of truancy conducted in schools in this country and one that allows for a large measure of confidence when we are extrapolating to state schools in general. In addition to this the Unit has also surveyed five inner-city schools, three of which were surveyed twice in successive academic years. Pupils surveyed in these schools ranged from Years 7 to 11. The results of these surveys, using a slightly modified questionnaire, are consistent with the main research, as is an earlier small-scale research project (covering three inner-city comprehensive schools) conducted by Stoll and O'Keeffe (1989).

The data gathered in these surveys point to the fact that in nearly all schools a significant number of pupils are truants. In the main survey conducted on behalf of the Department for Education, only three schools had truancy levels of 15 per cent or less and only one school (an all-girl selective school) had virtually no truancy problem.[1] Even the schools with the smallest truancy problem, then, have a sizeable number of pupils who absent themselves from school or lessons. At the other end of the continuum, 25 schools have truancy levels of 40 per cent or more, which suggests that one-sixth of all schools have very sizeable truancy problems. The mean truancy level for the 150 schools was 31 per cent, suggesting that typically nearly one-third of pupils truant in Years 10 and 11. When we look at Year 11 only, the picture is even gloomier. Fifty-nine schools had truancy levels above 40 per cent and 18 of these had levels in excess of 50 per cent. It is perhaps worth emphasising at this point that these are not 'problem' schools but schools chosen at random from English secondary schools in the state sector.

It is necessary to mention an obvious methodological problem at this point, one which strikes most people when they consider the problem of measuring truancy. How can truancy levels be measured if some of the intended objects of the study are likely to be absent? Ideally the researcher would return to each school, several times if necessary, to ensure that all pupils are surveyed. This proved impossible for financial reasons in the DfE-funded survey and so the statistics shown above are inevitably an underestimate of the full scale of the problem. The smaller-scale surveys did collect data over more than one visit and suggested even higher truancy levels, although it must also be realised that these surveys were conducted in mainly inner-city schools. The smaller-scale survey suggested that truancy levels for Year 10 and 11 pupils are around 47 per cent and that truancy levels are also significant in Years 7 (14 per cent), 8 (31 per cent) and 9 (31 per cent).

There were important methodological differences between the large survey and the smaller survey. In addition to the smaller survey being conducted in inner-city schools in one area of the country, a larger proportion of the pupils was surveyed (through repeat visits) and pupils were asked whether they had truanted since the beginning of the school year instead of during a single half-term period.

The most conservative estimate, then, for truancy levels is about 31 per cent for pupils in Years 10 and 11. This figure is based on the survey of 150 schools. There are good theoretical reasons to suppose that this may underestimate the true level. Inner-city schools appear to have higher mean levels of truancy even after allowing for methodological differences between surveys.

The above figures take into account only the question of whether pupils truant at some point in a given time-frame. Regular truancy is also a major problem. Nearly a half of the pupils who truanted did so several times each month. A large caveat needs to be added to this. Because of the methodological problem mentioned above, this is likely once again to underestimate the size of the problem. Put simply, the more frequently the pupil truants, the more likely it becomes that he will not be surveyed. The extent of the truancy problem is summarised in Table 6.1. All figures are taken from *Truancy in English Secondary Schools*.

Table 6.1   Truancy levels and frequency

	Truants %	Regular truants %
Year 10	25	9
Year 11	36	17
Both	31	14

Comparing truancy levels of girls and boys

Overall, boys truant slightly more than girls. This difference, however, is very small and masks much variation in the truancy patterns of boys and girls. In Year 11 the truancy levels among boys are significantly, but not spectacularly, higher than for girls (38 per cent compared to 31 per cent). Although the difference is clear enough it does little to reinforce the traditional view that truancy is mainly a male phenomenon. In Year 10 girls truant slightly more than boys although the difference is one of slightly less than one per cent (26 per cent to 25 per cent). Overall boys were only slightly more likely to truant than girls and this effect becomes statistically insignificant when the effects of single-sex schools are allowed for (single-sex boys' schools have higher than average levels, all-girl schools have lower than average levels). As is normal when one is dealing with large samples, the overall picture masks many variations. Some schools had high levels for boys and low levels for girls. In other schools this pattern was reversed. In some schools the pattern for Year 10 was the opposite of that for Year 11.

The small-scale research undertaken by the Truancy Unit, since the large DfE-funded sample, has suggested further variations in the differences between male and female truancy. These results confirm the trend shown above for Years 10 and 11, with girls truanting slightly less than boys and male truancy increasing more sharply in Year 11. For Years 7 to 9, however (not included in the major research programme), truancy levels among girls generally outstrip those for boys, in some instances by large amounts. Because of the small scale of this research (three mixed-sex schools) these results must be considered to be volatile but they clearly challenge the traditional assumption (often implicit rather than explicit) that truants are male.

Truancy is not confined to inner cities

It may be that truancy is a bigger problem in inner-city areas. This accords with common sense and the Truancy Unit has found truancy levels in some inner-city schools to be higher than in the schools surveyed for the Department for Education.

If this is true, and the evidence is not conclusive, it is, never-theless, certainly not the case that truancy is a problem only in the inner cities. The DfE-funded survey showed consistently high truancy levels in rural, suburban and industrial areas. Urban decline may fuel truancy but this must remain speculation until hard evidence can be brought forward. Poverty indicators, for example the proportion of pupils entitled to free school meals, did not correlate very significantly with truancy levels.

Truancy is often subject-specific

No subjects are immune from truancy, but some lessons are more susceptible than others. In the national survey, of all pupils who truanted and studied mathematics, 19 per cent said that they truanted to avoid this subject. This was not necessarily the sole reason given for truancy or the only lesson from which the pupil truanted. Indeed, many pupils truanted in order to avoid a range of lessons. It was clear, however, that pupils were making decisions on which parts of the curriculum they wanted to avoid. The corresponding percentages for the other key National Curriculum subjects of English and science were about the same at 18 per cent and 19 per cent respectively. Although no subjects had markedly lower truancy levels than this, some were clearly less popular or more prone to truancy. Games and physical education had 34 per cent of truants (who should be studying the subject) avoiding this subject in particular. This may be due in part to an increased opportunity for truancy in this subject—off-site activities may well offer increasing occasions for going missing, and feigned injuries or illness can often fool either teacher or parent into excusing a pupil from this subject. French (27 per cent), with no such obvious escape routes, was also markedly more susceptible to truancy, as were other modern languages. These truancy figures for individual subjects are shown in Table 6.2.

Table 6.2   Proportion of
truants truanting to avoid a
particular lesson

	%
English	18
French	27
Geography	16
History	19
Mathematics	19
PE/games	34
RE	20
Science	19
Technology	16

Base: truants who study the given
subject

These figures are across the 150 schools in the survey. What they mask is the variation from school to school. Truancy levels for particular subjects in individual schools and individual year groupings varied from negligible to accounting for the bulk of all subject truancy. This may partly reflect the various levels of supervisory control exercised over pupils but it is still clear that *what* is on offer significantly affects truancy levels and patterns. In the light of the DfE-funded survey into truancy, the question is not so much whether there is a link between curriculum and truancy but how strong the connection is.[2]

Truants are not as disaffected as is often supposed

It might be supposed that the truant is generally disillusioned by the school experience. Indeed, this is often an implicit assumption made when people are discussing truancy. Although this disillusionment is true of some truants it is not legitimate to generalise it to all truants. Half of all truants said that they truanted because of a dislike of school compared with two-thirds who truanted to avoid a particular lesson or lessons. (Many gave both reasons to explain their truancy.) In itself, this suggests that the overall experience of school is not as powerful a deterrent to attending as particular parts of the curriculum. However, when those truants who gave dislike of school as a reason for truancy were invited to identify why they disliked school, only 23 per cent answered that school was generally oppressive. This compares with 47 per cent of these pupils who identified a dislike of either particular subjects or teachers. Overall, only 11 per cent of all pupils found school to be generally boring or oppressive and only five per cent gave this as the sole reason for truancy. By comparison, 19 per cent of all truants gave the desire to avoid particular lessons as their sole reason for truancy.

More evidence that truants are, typically, not generally dis-affected comes from comparisons between the attitudes of truants and non-truants. All pupils were asked whether they found school enjoyable, whether they thought that what they were learning would be useful and if they wanted to continue their education when they were free to leave school.

As would be expected non-truants tended to find their subjects to have more utility value than truants, but the difference is less than might be supposed. Over a half of truants (54 per cent) thought that all or most of what they learned would be useful compared to 71 per cent for non-truants. Only one in five truants thought that what they learned would be mostly or totally useless. It is clearly sad that 20 per cent of truants (and eight per cent of non-truants) should feel that what they are being taught is of little value but it is also clear that perceived usefulness does not play a major role in determining truancy levels.

This is reinforced by the fact that when the 150 schools in the survey are rank-ordered by the percentage of pupils finding their subjects useful or mostly useful, there is no significant correlation with truancy levels. The 25 schools with the highest proportion of pupils finding their lessons useful had a mean truancy level of 28.9 per cent. This compared to 30.5 per cent for the 25 schools with the lowest proportion and the middle 100 schools actually had higher mean truancy levels than this at 31.6 per cent.

Similar results were found when pupils were asked if they enjoyed school. One-third of truants found school to be mostly or always enjoyable and another one-third were neutral. Again non-truants were more likely to enjoy school with 50 per cent saying school was enjoyable most or all of the time. Truants again have, in general, a greater tendency not to enjoy their schooling than their non-truanting friends. But most pupils, whether truants or not, find school at least tolerable.

When pupils were asked if they wanted to continue their education, 58 per cent of truants and 75 per cent of non-truants said yes. Seventeen per cent of truants said no compared to nine per cent of non-truants with the remaining pupils being undecided.

Again it seems that most pupils who truant are not alienated from the process of education although they may find parts of it unsatisfactory. A summary of the findings for this question are shown in Table 6.3.

Table 6.3   Would you like to continue education?

	Truants %	Non-truants %
Yes	58	75
No	17	9
Don't know	25	18

It seems from the measures of utility, enjoyment and desire to continue with education that about one-fifth of truants are significantly alienated from school. Although this is clearly a cause for concern, it cannot furnish more than a partial explanation of truancy, as 80 per cent of truants appear either to endorse the process of schooling and education or at least to be tolerant of it.

In contrast to this, truancy levels are highest where truancy is easiest—regardless of the perceived benefits of education. The 25 schools with the largest proportion of pupils reporting that truancy is easy had mean truancy levels 9 per cent higher than the 25 schools which were perceived as being most vigilant by pupils (34 per cent compared to 26 per cent). Two things are worth noting here. First, large numbers of pupils will truant given the chance in virtually all schools. Second, even the more attentive schools have significant truancy levels.

Summary of main statistical findings

Before we consider the implications of the findings of the University of North London Truancy Unit, it is worth recapping the main points above. Truancy is a significant phenomenon in nearly all state schools. Girls truant in very nearly equal numbers to boys. Inner-city schools may have higher mean truancy levels than other schools but all locations have levels of around 25 per cent or more. Truants often truant to avoid particular lessons and some lessons are more vulnerable than others. Only about one-fifth of all truants are completely alienated from school or the process of education; most truants accept a good deal of it and some endorse education or schooling as something that is clearly desirable. In spite of this many pupils will truant given the opportunity.

The truant and crime

How strong is the link between truancy and crime? The government is clearly committed to the belief that it is substantial—both the Home Office and the Department for Education have announced measures to break this link and they are not alone in emphasising the connection between crime and truancy. The supposed link between truancy and crime has already spawned much public policy but this link has only been tentatively and superficially established. The Department for Education, however, has chosen (it seems) to ignore its own commissioned research which points strongly to the fact that truancy is a far more extensive phenomenon than can be explained by a model of truancy based on criminality.

There clearly is some link between truancy and crime. The question is, or at least should be, what is the nature of this link and is it causal or incidental? Many criminals and young offenders are, or have been, truants. On the strength of this evidence alone it seems to be assumed that there is a natural progression from truanting to petty crime.

This assumption can be seen in the following statement from Home Office minister Michael Jack: 'There is a link between truancy and the tendency to commit crime and it is vital . . . that pupils attend school on a regular basis.' (*The Guardian*, 1993.)

It is no doubt proper for a Home Office minister to focus on the truancy/crime link as he is not primarily or professionally interested in the educational aspects of truancy but in its public order implications. It is strange, however, that Mr Patten should also have been more interested in this aspect of truancy when his first priority should, as Secretary of State for Education, surely have been in the implications for education policy. Announcing £500,000 of government money for local authorities to set up truancy watch schemes he stated: 'I am concerned about the link between truancy, poor academic performance and crime.' (*The Times*, 1993.)

It was also *The Times* that reported Mr Patten's white paper which dealt with truancy in the same manner: 'It [crime] starts with hanging around street corners, drifting into shoplifting and stealing bicycles, "progresses" to petty burglary, perhaps becoming involved with drugs . . . before long the journey from street corner to prison cell is complete.' (*The Times*, 1993.)

This probably describes the history of some truants but is it in any way typical? The evidence seems to consist entirely of the findings of research conducted by Cambridge University that 48 per cent of juvenile offenders had been truants at school. Although this is an interesting and significant statistic, it does not remotely

establish that truancy is a cause of crime to the extent inferred by
Mr Patten's white paper. Indeed, this unsubstantiated assumption
would serve well as a paradigm case of bad social science. In itself,
the fact that 48 per cent of juvenile offenders had truanted at
school tells us little until this is compared to truancy levels in
general and placed in a conceptual framework.

More bad reasoning in a similar vein is provided by the authors
of the 1990 factsheet on truancy from TV-am (TV-am, 1990). In
its section entitled 'Truancy and crime' it states that: 'In the
United States, 60 per cent of the prison population and 85 per cent
of youths in juvenile correction facilities were truants from school.'

Here, no study has confirmed the influence of truancy, but it is
known that:

- '70 per cent of household burglaries are committed by youths
  under 17 years of age.'
- 'One-third of all criminal offences are committed by youths
  under 17 years of age.'
- 'One-third of all young men have a criminal record by the time
  they are 28 years old.'
- '50 per cent of all crimes recorded are conducted by men under
  21 years of age.'

I have quoted the entire section of this document dealing with
truancy and crime. We are invited, on the basis of research in a
different country and the fact that all too many young people
become involved in crime, to conclude that truancy is a major cause
of crime. This may be a particularly barren example but it does
illustrate the willingness to jump from truancy to crime with only the
most tenuous of attempts to link the supposed cause and effect.

The problem is, as is mentioned by the TV-am factsheet, that
there is very little research to go by. It does appear that many
criminals are or were truants but this is not inconsistent with the
possibility that there is only a weak causal link between truancy and
crime.

If 60 per cent of US prisoners were truants then this is of no
significance until it is known what proportion of US school
students truant. It is by no means impossible that in the poor
American inner cities 60 per cent truancy is quite normal. If this
does prove to be the case then the prison population may simply
reflect the general incidence of truancy. There would in this case be
no evidence at all of a truancy–crime link (although it would not
disprove it either).

In this country, 48 per cent of juvenile offenders were truants
according to the research that so impressed John Patten. *Truancy in
English Secondary Schools* puts the truancy level for Year 10 and 11

pupils at 31 per cent. However, this is over a limited time-frame. Pupils were also asked if they had truanted in the previous year. When these pupils are added in, the percentage of pupils who truant at some time (over a period of a little more than a year) rises to 42 per cent. This figure is consistent with the smaller-scale surveys conducted by the University of North London Truancy Unit which suggest truancy levels of around 47 per cent for some inner-city schools.

It may well be then that truancy levels for young offenders are only marginally higher than for the general school population. Even if the figure of 31 per cent is taken as the general truancy level, however, it is still invalid to conclude that there is a strong link between truancy and crime. Even if criminals are more likely to have truanted than non-criminals, this does not demonstrate that truancy is a cause of crime. These young offenders have shown a rejection of society's values by acts of theft or in some cases violence. It is hardly surprising that young people who so radically reject general values should also indulge in the relatively trivial act of defiance by truanting from school. In some cases the act of truancy may have led to crime but it is hardly a convincing model as an explanation for youth crime. Perhaps it is more surprising that more young offenders are not truants. The fact that so many young offenders do not truant may suggest that truancy is not seen as a wrong act in any meaningful sense by young people. The link between truancy and crime would then be casual rather than causal. Truancy is typically a rational act. Truants miss lessons for rational reasons, usually to avoid parts of the curriculum which are perceived to be of little benefit. It may be that some young people miss school in order to create opportunities for petty crime but it seems perverse to say in this case that the truancy caused the crime.

Any convincing research on the truancy–crime link would have to show that acts of truancy lead to criminal acts in a significant number of instances. The research done so far has not looked at what truants do when they miss school but at whether young offenders have truanted. The research done for the DfE did ask students why they truanted and the majority were able to give rational explanations based on their perception of their experience at school. There was no evidence that their truancy was motivated by the opportunity to engage in crime.

Until such evidence is produced the theory that truancy and crime are strongly linked must be at best highly tentative. The best that can be hoped for by defenders of the truancy–crime link is that it might explain a small aspect of truancy. As a general explanatory model, it is of little use as it is unable to account for important known facts. If truants generally went on to commit crime then the number of female young offenders should be about the same as for males as is the case for truancy levels. However, young male offenders (convicted or cautioned) account for 78 per cent of all offences committed by young people aged between 14 and 17. In 1992, 80,000 males in this age range were cautioned or convicted for summary or indictable offences, compared to 22,000 females (*Annual Abstract of Statistics*, 1994).

The deficit model of truancy

This model for truancy is dealt with more fully in Chapter 3, on truancy and the curriculum. It is, however, worth noting that, as with the previously considered model, it does not sit well with the known facts about truancy.

Although the model is implicit rather than explicit, truants are generally seen to be lacking in some way either emotionally or intellectually. This may well be true of the one-fifth of all truants who seem to reject the whole process of schooling. Unlike the crime–truancy link, this model has some general explanatory power. The problem is that it really only applies to about 20 per cent of all truants and so misses the extent of the problem. Truancy is identified with the relatively small subset of all pupils who cannot cope with the process of schooling. It misses the majority of truants who reject school, or more typically parts of the curriculum for well-defined, rational reasons.

It can be saved as a model for some aspects of truancy but must fail as a general explanatory theory. It cannot explain how so many truants enjoy much of their schooling, find much of it useful and want to continue their education. Nor can it suggest plausible reasons why pupils often direct their truancy at particular lessons or school sessions.

One interesting and surprising fact that came to light after the report *Truancy in English Secondary Schools* was published is that there is no correlation between Year 11 truancy levels and the published examination performances for the schools surveyed. This is not consistent with the view that truancy is closely linked to poor academic performance, again suggesting that this model for truancy only explains minor aspects of the truancy phenomenon. The model of truancy as a rational act, however, does not presuppose that truancy would necessarily lead to poor academic performance. Truancy is not typically aimed at large enough sections of the curriculum to show significantly in examination performance. Truants miss small parts of the curriculum on certain occasions. If their truancy is rational then their absence will have no effect on their performance as the subject truanted from will either be one that the truant already knows is of no use or one that the truant has decided he or she can afford to miss at least on some occasions.

Conclusion

Truancy is a complex social phenomenon and it is not likely to be fully explained by any one conceptual model. Previous models, however, approached the problem from the wrong direction and thus missed the size of the problem. Earlier scholars, noticing that many criminals are or were truants, assumed that truancy has a major causal connection with crime. The problem is approached from the wrong end, reasoning in the wrong direction, and finishes up by concentrating on a minor manifestation of truancy.

The same fault is true of the deficit view of truancy. The most visible group of truants is likely to consist of truants who are unable to cope with the demands of schooling. These pupils' complete alienation from school is likely to show up as blatant and unsophisticated truancy. The problem is that if we concentrate on this obvious form of truancy, the full scale of truancy is masked. Truancy is taken to be evident and so the more sophisticated forms of truancy, about 80 per cent of all truancy, may easily go undetected. Truancy is then taken to be a much smaller problem than it actually is and the nature of truancy and the truant is misunderstood. A much fuller picture of truancy is given by treating truancy as a sophisticated form of curriculum rejection. If truants are taken to be rational then the old view of truancy as a relatively small-scale problem centred on inadequate or deviant children gives way to a model that can explain the fact that truancy is widespread but selective.

Notes

1. The truancy level, as measured in the survey, is the relative frequency of pupils who truant at least once during a half-term period.
2. For a fuller discussion on the statistical link between curriculum and truancy see Chapter 3, on truancy and the curriculum.

References

Annual Abstract of Statistics 1994 (1994) HMSO.
The Guardian (1993) 9 January.
'Missing Out' (1990) TV-am.
O'Keeffe, D.J. (1994) *Truancy in English Secondary Schools*, HMSO.
Stoll, P. and O'Keeffe, D.J. (1989) *Officially Present; An investigation into post-registration truancy in nine maintained schools*, Institute of Economic Affairs.
The Times (1993) 4 March.
The Times (1994) 9 February.

7 Truancy in English secondary schools: some lessons for the Educational Welfare Service

Dennis O'Keeffe

Summary of argument

Educational Welfare Officers (EWOs) need not abandon their long-term interest in children for whom school is difficult and threatening, because of their troubled home backgrounds etc. There always have been such children and there always will be presumably. What EWOs will need to do in the light of current reorganisation of ancillary educational services, however, is to show a greater interest than before in 'mainstream' truancy. Mainstream truancy may be understood as that truancy which recent evidence shows to have its origin mainly in dissatisfaction with lessons, i.e. the truancy in question has a rational and pondered basis. Rejection of lessons is not the only reason for truancy; but it is by far the most important. It is especially significant in the phenomenon of post-registration truancy (PRT) in which children officially present in school deliberately cut lessons. Lesson dissatisfaction is also the biggest factor in blanket truancy (BT), which involves children's staying away from school completely for periods of half a day or more, though in general BT is not as lesson-sensitive as PRT. Given that truancy relates overall more to lesson dissatisfaction than to any other influence, however, EWOs would do well to make sure that their expertise includes intimate familiarity with problems of curriculum, lessons and teaching. The status and future of EWOs will be the more secure to the extent that they become experts on the truancy of otherwise perfectly normal and rule-abiding pupils, who are the majority of truants.

The recent reorganisation of certain aspects of the work of ancillary educational services in this country may have occasioned justifiable complaint and resentment. Whatever the case, it is necessary now for the Educational Welfare Service in some degree to rethink its role in the securing of high educational standards.

One possible strategy is for the service to reconsider at some length its potential as an arm in the battle against truancy. That officers should try to encourage attendance and discourage truancy is not new. It has long been a central part of their function. However, the recently published report on truancy by the University of North London perhaps supplies a propitious occasion to quicken the process of rethinking (O'Keeffe, 1994).

The findings of the report are of huge general and specific interest to Educational Welfare Officers. First, its scale, nearly 38,000 Year 10 and 11 pupils having completed the confidential questionnaires which were the main research instrument of the project, is such as to transcend any earlier findings or preconceptions as to the nature of and reasons for the phenomenon of truancy.

Our report makes much of the central distinction between blanket truancy (not coming to school, deliberately, and without justification) and post-registration truancy, which is the deliberate cutting of lessons by people who have registered at school. The distinction between the two is not novel; but this is the first major report to make it a central aspect of the research involved.

The results show that there are far more acts of PRT than of BT, though most truants do both. More significant is that PRT is more sensitive to discontent with lessons than is BT, though both are more sensitive to lesson dissatisfaction than to any other single variable, and both become more sensitive to lesson dissatisfaction at higher frequencies of commission.

The clear implication is that EWOs need to become well informed in the matter of PRT and in the matter of the links between truancy of either type and the curriculum. EWOs should henceforth be increasingly aware of those influences on attendance and truancy which arise from the interior life of the school rather than from psychological deficits in schoolchildren themselves.

About one-third of the pupils surveyed admitted to truanting,[1] and they seem for the main part to share most of the outlook of the educational mainstream. They seem not to reject school in general. They find most of the curriculum useful. Most of them want to continue their education beyond the minimum leaving age. Though many truants dislike individual teachers they rarely claim that teachers take insufficient interest in their learning. Moreover, though there are truants who say that their parents and teachers know that they truant, there are far larger numbers of non-truants who say that among their reasons for not truanting anxiety about parental or school displeasure if they are found out predominates.

Over two-thirds of all truants say that one of their reasons for truanting is that they dislike certain lessons; and a fifth of all truants say that such dislike is the only reason for their truanting. This demonstration of the extreme importance of lessons in the minds of teenagers deciding whether to go to them or not, may in time come to be understood as one of the principal findings of modern empirical sociology of education. It would be well worth the while of EWOs to investigate the problems *vis-à-vis* attendance which seem to afflict the least popular subjects on the curriculum among pupils in Years 10 and 11: PE/games; French; mathematics; English, Obviously our data suggest that some lessons are inadequate for one reason or another. While it would not be appropriate to approve of pupils' deciding to engage in illegal absence, we think that some attention to the problem of improving the lessons in question in some way is clearly called for.

EWOs would be well advised to familiarise themselves with the various strategies for improving attendance. One obvious consideration is of the things which make for a school's being a welcoming place. Schools like White Hart Lane, in Haringey, have made notable reductions in truancy by paying attention to this crucial aspect of school. Our survey showed, however, that even children who esteem most of their lessons are quite likely to cut them if school is slack. Those schools which are vigilant have lower levels of truancy than those which are not. Human nature, it seems, is the same in school as it is elsewhere.

EWOs might advisedly inform themselves in a three-pronged strategy for reducing truancy:

1. Improving the quality of lessons.
2. Improving the level of vigilance.
3. Improving the welcoming aspects of school.

In particular a detailed knowledge of curricular matters is called for. Some truants say that they cut classes because the subject in question is too hard. Our speculation here, and it cannot be more than speculation, is that this might prove of lesser significance if their earlier preparation in primary or secondary school had been more thorough. In any event, it would seem that EWO training ought to include some intimate knowledge of the primary/ secondary link, including the intellectual aspects of the link, in the context of varying propensities to attend and to truant. Today's truancy may be the learning-failure of five or ten years back.

When pupils were invited to write freely about their reasons for cutting lessons or truanting from school if they did so, a minority of truants mentioned home difficulties. If a concentration on home difficulties has constituted a main element in the work of EWOs to date, then the concentration may have been wrong, but not the idea itself. Our result surely indicates that this aspect of understanding truancy still has claims on our attention, however much larger other influences on truancy may be. Home difficulties will remain something EWOs must know about.

Even here we must be careful. There is no general evidence in our report to the effect that those who speak of difficulties in the home are necessarily people of inadequate character or temperament. Perhaps in-depth interviewing of the kind that was not possible for us to carry out given the scale of our sample, would reveal patterns of psychological unpreparedness *vis-à-vis* school. We do not know. What we do know is that if there are children whose truancy can be seen as reflecting a 'pathological' deficit, they seem to be very much in a minority.

If, in the event, EWOs have indeed been encouraged to relate the truancy problem mainly to home background, the research findings should largely dissuade them from this view. It is not that home influences are not important. It would be blatant nonsense to suggest that they are not. Nor, sadly, is it the case that there are no deficient homes. It is moreover true, as was pointed out by Principal Education Welfare Officer Beryl Radford, from Bradford LEA, who served on the DfE steering committee for our report, that if you interviewed in depth some of the children who say they truant mainly because of dislike of lessons, you might well uncover deep personal and background problems, which also explain, or even alternatively explain, the phenomenon in question.

The authors of the present report would not disagree with Beryl Radford in principle on this issue. She may well be right. But one does not have to be possessed of positivistic zeal to want to stay as close to the available evidence as possible. This means confining our analysis and speculation largely to the responses of pupils to the questionnaires we gave them. It would not in any case be possible to conduct in-depth interviews on the scale of our sample. Nor is it clear how one would operationalise such research in a way

yielding systematic information about the motives for truancy. All
in all, to ask children to fill in questionnaires as to why they do or
do not truant, seems likely to yield more coherent and tractable
information than any other procedure. Their confidential answers
may present all sorts of difficulty; but they come as close to genuine
data as one is likely to be able to get.

The point in need of emphasis is that in most cases truants'
answers do not suggest a pathological deficiency in the children
themselves. While it is also true that most of their answers do not
suggest that school as an institution is generally dysfunctional
either, it is nevertheless the case, as we have seen, that the evidence
upholds the contention that if there is a pathology in relation to
truancy it may more readily be sought in the curriculum than in the
personalities of children. Dislike of lessons on the grounds that
they are irrelevant or boring or too difficult, or alternatively that the
homework which goes with them is too burdensome or the people
who teach them are not likeable—this amorphous phenomenon
vastly surpasses any other influence on truancy. It needs a lot more
research and attention, in this country and abroad.

While it is sad that children truant in large numbers, there is
also a message of hope to be drawn from our research. Secondary
school is not unpopular with the children of this country. The
results from our survey questionnaires most certainly do not
suggest a widespread alienation from school and its purposes on
the part of many English teenagers, even when they engage in
frequent truancy.

Nor do our results bear out the often claimed centrality of some
of the more exotic forms of modern educational discourse. Truants
do not complain about sexism or racism (i.e. these were not
reasons they gave for truanting). Rather few cited bullying as a
significant reason for non-attendance, though in this last case two
per cent did say that consideration was involved. In the case of
sexism and racism, despite their extraordinary prominence in
educational discussion, the issues in our case did not even reach
the statistical map, so little did they figure in our respondents'
answers. If we are right that these questions are overblown in our
educational life, and if this is reflected in the training of
Educational Social Workers, then perhaps a rethink is due on the
way educational social work is taught. We are quite certain,
incidentally, that these topics have been given much too much
exposure in teacher education.

Our results simply do not offer any late comfort for the now
largely interred neo-Marxist tradition in the sociology of
education, which a few years back supplied a theoretical
underpinning for these concerns. There is little in the data

uncovered in this survey to support the notion of children as oppressed victims of an exploitative order. The part that neo-Marxist theory once played in teacher education has now virtually evaporated. It is widely alleged today that it survives in social work training. If it also survives at all in the training of Educational Welfare Officers, it does not deserve to in terms of what children themselves say about school, sex, race, etc. Most children, including most truants, do not see themselves as hard done by or as victims. If some do, then their plight should not be taken as a general measure of how things are in our schools. It is not helpful to public policy to make the wayward or the unusual serve as the norm for analysis or debate. This is why we have taken issue with certain leading politicians who insist on the links between truancy and crime. Truancy is illegal; the reasons for linking it with crime as such seem to us simply absent.

Thus it is with questions of race and sex. On the overblown study of race in the educational context, we would refer readers to the report by David Smith and Sally Tomlinson (1989), in which they admit that the evidence of widespread perception of racism on the part of racial minorities, an evidence which they expected would be manifest, was simply not forthcoming.

None of this is to say that there might not be different propensities to truancy as between different ethnic groups. We do not know and advisedly we did not ask pupils for any racial self-identification on their questionnaires. The children were asked to identify themselves as boys and girls. The results here show overall little difference. Year 10 girls truant a bit more than boys; in Year 11 there is noticeably more truancy among the boys, though the difference is not huge. This is not to say that there is no sexual or racial prejudice in schools; but clearly such as there is does not manifest itself in a sense of harassment since it does not drive children to truancy.

In the event, much more significant than any difference between male and female truancy, is the huge jump in truancy between Years 10 and 11, an increase of 11 per cent between the Year 10 figure of 25 per cent and the Year 11 figure of 36 per cent. Since Year 11 is the critical year of public examinations, this finding reinforces our general contention that truancy is pre-eminently a curricular phenomenon. It is apparent that there is a frightening increase in lesson rejection at this time.

Though we believe our research has broken new ground, there is clearly a lot we do not know and a lot more work to be done to fill in the gaps in our ignorance. In particular we need to know how far bad attendance in Years 10 or 11, or earlier, relates to an inadequate curriculum lower down the system. This is a question in whose elucidation research sociologists and EWOs might fruitfully co-operate.

Notes

1. Our research window was a rather narrow one. We asked the pupils about truancy in the previous half-term. When they are asked about longer periods the figures are much higher. This was the case in our new report when we asked the children in a supplementary question if they had truanted the previous year. This took the level up to more than 40 per cent. It seems that truancy is fluid and that in some cases people stop and start in unpredictable ways. There is probably a higher level of truancy in the summer term, a consideration which needs investigation.

References

O'Keeffe, D.J. (1994) *Truancy in English Secondary Schools*, HMSO.
Smith, D.J. and Tomlinson, S. (1989) *The School Effect: A Study of Multi-Racial Comprehensives*, Policy Studies Institute.

8 Training courses for improving attendance

Patricia Stoll

Introduction

During the three years that the Truancy Unit at the University of North London has existed, an expertise in the training of those personnel—teachers, Education Social Workers (ESWs), Education Welfare Officers (EWOs), Heads of Special Units, GEST fund holders and others—who have a special interest in and a responsibility for attendance and truancy has been developed.

In response to the announcement by the Department for Education (DfE) in July 1992 that £10 million would be channelled into local education authorities (LEAs) in April 1993 as a part of Grants for Education Support and Training (GEST) funding, the Truancy Unit organised two-day in-service training courses directed at ways of improving attendance and curbing truancy. Although this funding is specifically for 'support' and 'training' we could find little evidence of the latter. We have become, therefore, pioneers in the field.

At the time of the announcement by the DfE the Unit had just completed a large study on truancy for the DfE which had involved 20 LEAs and 150 schools in mainland England. All pupils in Years 10 and 11 who were present on the day that the researchers visited the school completed an anonymous questionnaire. As a result almost 38,000 questionnaires were completed providing the Unit with a huge data base on pupils' truancy, attitudes to school and the curriculum and their aspirations and so on. This wealth of information provides the theoretical framework for the courses. The research team realised that, as a result of the work, they had a unique experience and expertise to offer in the form of intensive and in-depth training in the field of truancy.

The findings of the report do much to demolish the previously held concept that school is an unquestionable good and that anyone rejecting it is deviant. Truants were described as 'unhappy children', 'school phobics' and generally thought to be emotionally disturbed. Our work has shown that this is not the case. We are not saying that there are no truants who fit these descriptions. Clearly there are. What we are saying, however, is that the majority of pupils are not deviants but young people who have made a rational decision to stay away from school or lessons. Furthermore, we have also shown that although a number of pupils do truant from school *per se* the most common form of truancy among 14- to 16-year-olds is post-registration truancy. The main purpose of the training courses, therefore, is to present to teachers and education personnel a clear insight into truancy based on our findings and thus equip them with the expertise to deal with truancy as it occurs in their particular school or schools.

Training courses

There are a variety of courses that the Unit can offer. All, however, are concerned with improving attendance and combating truancy—in that order. The rationale of the courses is based on the belief that it is not possible to deal effectively with a problem unless there is a clear understanding of what is to be addressed. There is much ignorance about truancy and many misconceptions.

The first day of the course sets out to explore the concept of truancy and dispel some of the myths. For example, truancy is not confined only to a pupil's staying away from school when he or she has no good reason for not being there. Our research has shown that, certainly among Year 10 and 11 pupils, post-registration truancy (PRT) is the more common form of truancy. Here a boy or girl registers in school but fails to turn up at one or more lessons during the course of the day. On the whole it is blanket truancy (BT) or whole-day truancy that has been the concern of schools and the Education Welfare Service (EWS). This kind of truancy is more identifiable as the child is absent from school. Such truants are invariably referred to the EWS.

In the courses designed specifically for teachers, EWOs and ESWs we attempt to show, however, that there is a need for EWOs and ESWs to become involved in school with post-registration truants. It is our contention that much preventive work could be done if EWOs/ESWs were to have the opportunity to work with pupils in school in partnership with teachers. A school EWO might, for example, detect signs of curricular dissatisfaction in the early stages. The report showed quite clearly that the most common reason for truancy—both PRT and BT—among 14- to 16-year-olds was some form of dissatisfaction with the curriculum.

Various models of courses have been evolved—some designed to be held at the university and some to be held in a school or LEA Professional Centre. Each course is tailored to suit the particular audience. An outline of the different models is given below, each of which can easily be adapted to suit particular needs.

Course A: a two- or three-day course for educational personnel

This course is designed for inspectors, advisers, Chief Education Social Workers, Principal Education Welfare Officers and GEST fund holders.

Day 1

An in-depth look at truancy is provided. This comprises the different kinds of truancy—BT, PRT, 'near' truancy, opportunistic truancy—the reasons, the frequency and so on. The information is based on the findings of the report and our previous research studies and includes a major presentation of our most recent findings. Time is allowed for group discussion followed by a plenary session.

Day 2

The following are covered:

1. School-based research: the value to the school and LEA of a research programme tailored to suit the individual school and its needs. This will give those in authority an insight into truancy in their school, the nature of it and the frequency. It will undoubtedly indicate problem areas in the curriculum. A

school which is in possession of such information is in a very strong position to deal with the root causes of truancy.

2. The government truancy league tables: an examination and assessment of the tables which include defining 'authorised' and 'unauthorised' absence as well as advice on compiling the tables.

3. School-based strategies for improving attendance: a study of two schools' projects which can be adapted for use in other schools.

4. The roles of the LEAs and the EWS in matters of attendance and truancy. Practical ways in which EWOs and ESWs can work with pupils in school, as well as continuing to liaise with home and school, are put forward.

5. Presentations of the state-of-the-art electronic registration systems.

Course B: a two-day course for teachers and education welfare service personnel

Day 1

Truancy: an exploration of the concept of truancy and its manifestations based on the findings of the report. The day includes a major presentation of the findings and the opportunity for group discussion. The day closes with a plenary session.

Day 2

The focus of the second day is on improving school attendance. There is a presentation of two school models, School A and School B. School A had substantial funding over a three-year period to improve the rate of attendance in the school. School B decided to tackle truancy in the school by tightening up discipline and security in the building as well as making some curricular innovations. This was achieved with very little funding. One member of staff, the head of special needs, was partially funded from the authority's GEST budget.

The school presentations are followed up by discussion on how the ideas and strategies can be adapted for the needs of the schools represented by those attending the course.

A further presentation based on the 'Cities in Schools' model is given. Here, a 'unit' is set up in a school for hard-core truants. This project is somewhat limited as it is designed entirely for blanket truants. The organisers have not yet acknowledged the problem of

PRT and the needs of those particular truants. There is scope for widening such a project to include pupils who come to school but truant from particular lessons. Many of these pupils are hard-core truants for there are some lessons that many of them *never* attend.

The purpose of the 'Cities in Schools' model is to provide a sanctuary for pupils who cannot cope with mainstream school for whatever reason. The work involves not only providing education in school for pupils who would not be receiving any form of schooling but also liaising with the home and attempting to address any problems there through such agencies as social welfare. The project is viewed as a short-term strategy as the overall objective is to reintegrate the pupil into mainstream school. It is too early yet to make an assessment of the success or otherwise of the projects. The model does, however, have an appeal for some schools such as those that have a significant BT problem.

The presentation includes an examination of four case studies of truants. The course members are divided into four groups with each group discussing at some length one of the case studies. The discussion covers an assessment of the particular truant and how she or he can best be helped. The value of such an exercise depends largely on the particular experiences and involvement with truancy of the participants. It is, for example, popular with EWOs and ESWs and those teachers who are working in inner-city schools where, as our report showed, the incidents of BT are higher.

Much attention has been paid recently to truancy by the media, and as a result there is a great deal of interest in the phenomenon among educationalists, academics and the police—the latter because of the tentative link with juvenile crime. We believe there is a case for providing more intensive courses for those wishing to undertake research in their schools or LEAs or areas as well as those wishing to do a higher degree. Such a course would comprise one day—or a half-day—per week for a six-week, or longer, period of time. The aim of the course would be to provide a much deeper insight into truancy, the curriculum and school ethos. A considerable component would be the study of research methods and practical training in the organisation of a research project. There would be training in the setting up of a data base, the processing of data and report writing. This would be an academic course with the possibility of some form of certification on successful completion.

Conclusion

Teachers, Education Welfare Service personnel, LEA officers and others who have responsibility for pupils' attendance at school need to receive the training necessary to enable them to carry out their duties effectively. I have shown here how we have the experience to provide such training. Too many schools at present are content to put all their energies into addressing BT so that they can produce satisfactory attendance tables. As a result too often PRT is ignored. Schools which avail themselves of the facts about truancy are in a strong position not only to improve attendance but also to deal with truancy, both BT and PRT.

Part III
Further vistas

9 Truancy and crime

Dennis O'Keeffe

How are truancy and juvenile crime and deviancy connected? It is quite clear that they correlate statistically, though only in a small minority of cases. Most pupils are not truants in any significant sense. Most truants are not criminals. Indeed, some criminals are not truants. But even were the lines of correlation stronger than they are, that is to say if most truants were demonstrably criminal, it would not follow that the crime had any causal connection with the truancy. It is after all a first rule of causal investigation that correlation is not explanation. The tendency of truants to become criminal might have its causes in factors quite outside school. In other words, the truancy and the criminality might both be dependent variables caused by independent factors having little connection with school, save that the moral function of school was not successful in these cases, since the criminality nevertheless occurred.

The University of North London's recent work on truancy (O'Keeffe, 1994), commissioned by the DfE, did not have a remit to investigate crime or delinquency. The report, however, does throw some oblique light on the question. It produced a very mixed picture. There are worrying levels of truancy and a good many lessons are regarded as unsatisfactory by the pupils required to attend them. That one in three pupils admitted to at least one act of truancy in the six weeks we asked them about is very disturbing. Moreover, a large minority do a lot of truancy. Among 16-year-olds on our study, ten per cent said they truant at least once a week.

On the other hand the report showed very clearly that the grounds for thinking most truants are alienated from school are very slender. Most children, and most truants, like school, approve of most of the curriculum and want to stay on after the minimum leaving age. There appears to be no mass alienation from school in this country among young people of 15 and 16, of whom nearly 38,000 completed our truancy questionnaires. The view, often repeated by leading educational politicians, that truancy promotes crime, is an example of the dangers of common sense projected too readily onto the field of complex social phenomena.

The idea that truancy will inexorably promote crime rests on two errors. The first is that the truant is inadequate, deviant or criminal. The evidence suggests that this is simply not so. The second is that school is an unproblematic good from which only the world's deviants could possibly recoil. This view is not sustainable either. We now know very well that schools in very similar socio-economic contexts have different moral atmospheres, different work ethos, different academic success and attendance levels. The individual school has a moral and intellectual life of its own, requiring analysis in its own right. Writers like Mortimore, Rutter and Cox and Marks have shown this in a way which now must surely be accepted as approaching the incontrovertible.

In this regard it would actually be surprising if school were *not* connected with deviancy and crime for a minority of pupils. The typical moral perception of today's individuals must be formed somewhere in the triad of home, school and entertainment. The key research and policy questions must concern the genesis and nature of youth culture. What (minority) portion of youth culture is criminal/deviant? How is that portion formed and what part does school play in it?

These questions break down into further refinements. We need to know whether juvenile crime relates more intimately to blanket truancy (staying away from school altogether for unspecified periods) or post-registration truancy. Common sense suggests that blanket truancy is the more likely culprit; but common sense is an uncertain guide. On the DfE research, for example, the authors fully expected to find that large schools promote more truancy than small, being less convivial places to work. This 'common sense' expectation was not borne out by the evidence.

We need to know much more about what truants do when they truant as well as where they go. This includes those large numbers of truants who do not even leave the school building when they truant. Some of the North American evidence of school-based crime suggests that the moral hazards of attendance may in extreme cases rival those of absence. Some of the most likely deviants may prefer to attend school, at least as far as registering in the morning or afternoon is concerned. Indeed, as suggested long ago by Paul Willis, they may even enjoy being in class.

In any event it is not helpful to throw around mechanistic associations when the appropriate evidence has not been gathered. We have to ask whether the propensities to crime or truancy are significantly formed in the primary school or whether it is the secondary school experience which is crucial. Nor do we know how the home, school and entertainment links operate. School can confirm a good home and reverse the influence of a bad one. But what of the agonising experience of good parents whose children go wrong during their school years? This might conceivably relate to a bad school experience. In any case it is at least possible that the video-nasty culture can overturn good homes and good schools.

Most interestingly of all, we need to know why girls seem to truant almost as much as boys and yet are much less given to deviancy or criminality. Our major research showed boys truanting rather more than girls in Year 11, but less in Year 10. Subsequent privately commissioned work done by us has confirmed this pattern. There are clearly urgent questions requiring careful, sensitive and systematic study. There seems little sense in pronouncing until we know more.

References

O'Keeffe, D.J. (1994) *Truancy in English Secondary Schools*, HMSO.

10 Truancy and the primary school

Dennis O'Keeffe and Patricia Stoll

One of the key findings in *Truancy in English Secondary Schools* (O'Keeffe, 1994) was the huge jump in truancy between Years 10 and 11. In subsequent confidential work, commissioned by secondary schools anxious about their truancy problem, we have found both confirming evidence of this phenomenon and parallel evidence that truancy is in general terms a rising function of compulsory secondary education, with levels worse in Year 8 than Year 7, in Year 9 than in 8, in 10 than in 9.

This is not to suggest that compulsion is a necessary component of truancy. Preliminary considerations suggest that truancy is very high in some FE colleges, among students who are in voluntary attendance. Perhaps, in an era of high juvenile unemployment, economic circumstances supply a dull surrogate of compulsion, that is to say that many students would not be enrolled in these institutions if the labour market were nearer full employment conditions. We do not know, though it is at least clear that voluntary attendance does not mean no truancy. Truancy is certainly not unknown, if equally certainly under-researched, among 'A' level students, though in our view this would not be tolerated in any decent academy. As for undergraduates, their truancy is notorious, both when attendance at lectures is voluntary and when it is compulsory.

Nothing definitive is being claimed here, then, about the sociology of compulsory attendance. It is clear, however, that compulsion as such must in some degree be an influence. We have shown, in the largest school-based study of truancy ever undertaken in this country, that there is a massive increase in the levels of this activity between Years 10 and 11. This must put compulsion on the research agenda.

The question then poses itself: what about the primary experience? Truancy is much lower at the start of secondary education than at the close. This suggests that the burden of compulsion is felt much more lightly by younger students. Maybe this pattern obtains also in the primary school. Is it likely that if one investigated truancy at the primary level it would be found to fade continuously as the investigative gaze moved downward between Years 6 and 1? Conceivably it might prove to be the case that with the little children in Years 1, 2 or 3, truancy is virtually non-existent.

Since very little is known about the sociology (or, indeed, about any theoretical aspects) of primary school attendance, we are operating to some extent in a speculative void. Teachers in primary school, as well as Educational Welfare Officers and Educational Social Workers, often say that there is quite a lot of blanket truancy from the primary school, mostly parent-condoned. They must be right, though there is no hard data to confirm their assertions. In any case it is reasonable to maintain that truancy is not especially acute at the primary stage. Certainly, suggestive hypotheses arise naturally enough.

There might, for example, be a better fit between the psychology of childhood and the primary curriculum than between the psychology of adolescence and the secondary curriculum. Perhaps, if 'play' as very broadly conceived is a larger component of the atmosphere of the primary school, then compulsion will seem less of an intrusion to the primary child than it does to the secondary pupil, expected as he or she is to engage in an academic curriculum.

Perhaps the supervisory ambience of the primary school is less irksome to children than that of the secondary school. The former reflects and echoes the highly personalised life of the home; the latter anticipates the more impersonal and bureaucratic world of adult work.

Perhaps, to put the matter more crudely and simply, children of primary age are inherently more biddable than older children. Perhaps also primary school is more enjoyable for most children than secondary school. Maybe these two factors work together, so that children become less tractable just when they are plunged into a more forbidding environment.

If this is the case, then the well-known 'culture shock' which some children experience during the move from primary school to secondary can be seen in a new light: that of its explanatory potential with regard to truancy, largely as a new or at any rate intensified problem.

One repeats that these are all speculations. Nor is it difficult to see that counterspeculations are also available. First it may not be the case that the curricular *lebenswelt* differs so much between the levels of schooling. One standard rejoinder to critics of progressive primary education is that it was never so fully instantiated as its enemies seemed to think. Even for those such as ourselves, who believe that there *is* a distinctive and influential progressive ideology typical of primary education and a more traditional conservatism typical of secondary education, it is not easy to divide all primary schools from all secondary ones along such lines. There are 'traditional' elements in many primary schools and 'progressive' elements in many secondary ones.

Radical and opposite hypotheses can easily be advanced. The progressive one would be that secondary children truant because secondary schools are often unpleasant and that high attendance can be encouraged only by the reformation of secondary schools on progressive lines. The alternative, traditional, hypothesis—which we favour—is that progressive education, however much it fits in with the play orientation of early childhood, systematically under-prepares the children passing through its ministrations for the rigours of secondary education.

None of us knows in any evidentially satisfactory way which of these two extremes is nearer the truth, though it may well be proper to appeal to circumstantial evidence, such as that supplied by the Adult Literacy and Basic Skills Unit, to the effect that millions of people have passed through compulsory education without achieving basic literacy or numeracy. That being the case, high levels of truancy in secondary schools would hardly seem surprising. In any event, there is a war going on for the souls of our children which, of great concern to us all, is of extreme interest to scholars of attendance and truancy.

The 'progressive'/'traditional' battle

The personnel and advocates of the different levels may, and do, seek converts in their adjacent levels or even further afield. There is talk in higher education these days, for example, of 'student-centred learning'—clear evidence, it seems to us, of an influence from the primary level operating at the tertiary. Indeed, the rise of the 'graduate only' policy for schoolteachers led, probably inevitably, to greater contact between the bottom and the top levels, just when the close articulation between primary and secondary levels was broken by the abolition of the 11-plus and the attendant diminution in downward academic pressure.

To say that there may be missionary movements between the different levels, is not, however, to say that these can be only from the primary, pupil-centred progressive mode as the inspiration and onto the secondary mode by way of conversion. On the contrary, one way of characterising the National Curriculum is to identify it as a mechanism for making primary schools more like secondary ones. Conservative governments since 1979 have been notably hostile to progressive education, though this is not to say they have done much to contain it. Indeed, more marked in national terms has been the reverse phenomenon at work. Some secondary schools have become distinctly more 'primary' in tone and organisation. The whole movement of the last 30 years, aimed at making secondary school more friendly and less forbidding, more relaxed and less demanding, has been part and parcel of the general move towards progressive culture. The huge determination by sizeable sections of the education establishment that secondary schools shall not be placed in 'raw' intellectual rank order, for example, is a clear rejection of the adult, work-orientated ethos which also pulls on the attention of the secondary school world.

In *Truancy in English Secondary Schools* we found that schools with tougher discipline had lower levels of truancy than the softer dispensations. The speculative jump here might be to the effect that the softer schools are not just softer but advisedly so, that they are those more touched by the progressive ideology. If this were the case, the progressive mode would, indeed, as we suspect, constitute part of the problem rather than part of the solution. We must stress, however, that our government-commissioned work affords no evidence that this is so. It is not the case, whatever our prejudices, that our official data show that worse discipline in secondary schools means more progressivism or vice versa. Common sense will suggest to any traditionally minded student of education that this is, indeed, likely to be the case; but the issue remains unsettled.

We have not hesitated to raise these difficult matters, nevertheless. The large and troubled question of the rival claims of 'progress' and 'tradition' in our maintained schools needed an airing, in the area of attendance/truancy as well as over the issue of intellectual standards. Research is needed to establish the shape of things. In any case, we are at least in a position to offer some rather more modest data for readers' inspection. We can say a little about the genesis of post-registration truancy, as this spans the primary and secondary levels.

Primary school truancy

We have already noted that truancy in primary schools has always been thought of in terms of blanket truancy. We have recently become aware, however, of a form of truancy in primary school having a close similarity to post-registration truancy in the secondary school: extended toilet visitation (ETV).

Recent privately commissioned research by us has led us to the view, interviewing some 40 secondary school children, that ETV is a normal feature of upper primary school experience, and one that has a close connection to the curriculum. Having earlier speculated about the possible reality of this phenomenon, in conversations with teachers and EWOs, we were invited by a secondary school in the home counties to test our hypothesis. This, however, was only as an incidental feature of other work that was demanded of us. The school wanted us to assess an attendance project that had been in place throughout the academic year.

This project was designed to improve attendance and increase awareness of lateness to and truancy from school or lessons. Its controllers were delighted when we asked to include questions about ETV in the primary school.

Assessing the project

We interviewed more than 40 pupils in the school from Years 7, 8, 9 and 10. We left out Year 11 because it was summertime and examinations were the priority for this Year. Our questions included one about primary school behaviour. The question was: When you were in the primary school did you ever go to the toilet and stay there for a while to miss some of the lesson?

There were 22 girls and 19 boys in the sample. We knew their Christian names, but did not record them on our data sheets. The pupils thus were guaranteed complete anonymity. They were able to speak freely, knowing that the results would be confidential.

ETV in the primary schools

Our results showed that primary school pupils do stay in the toilets for 10, 15 or even 20 minutes to avoid lessons which they find irksome. Twenty of our interviewees said they had done this, for this reason, mostly for between 15 and 20 minutes. Pupils specifically said that any longer time than this was likely to bring retribution. Sixteen of our pupils said they had not stayed in the toilets in primary school to miss lessons, and four said they could not remember. These four were all in Year 10, a year beginning to be rather distant from the primary experience.

Our results nevertheless convinced us that with children in the early years of secondary school memories of ETV in the primary school will remain vivid. From the point of view of research such memories constitute a very useful empirical handle on attendance in the primary school. Though the numbers in our sample were small, their answers to the other questions we asked them, questions based on our work *Truancy in English Secondary Schools*, were notably consistent with our government findings. This general consistency seemed to us good grounds for treating their answers on ETV in the primary school as trustworthy.

We fully recognise that ETV may continue to happen in secondary schools. What we insist on, is that wherever it occurs, it is a form of post-registration truancy. In any case, it seems at least likely that the habit of absenting oneself from large parts of the curriculum is well established among children in the upper part of primary school. This may greatly facilitate the habit of post-registration truancy in the secondary school.

ETV and its potential policy implications

It is evident that systematic work would have to be done to establish whether our small-scale sample is anything like typical of behaviour in the primary schools of this country. Our interviewees' responses to questions about secondary truancy were very close to those we found in our large-scale DfE work; so in principle we were inclined to be impressed by their answers about the primary school. It does look as if there may well be a continuity in the impulse pupils feel to absent themselves, across the whole range of upper primary and secondary education. One possible policy implication is to the effect that successful diminution of the level of ETV in the primary school may establish good habits of classroom attendance in the secondary school.

References

O'Keeffe, D.J. (1994) *Truancy in English Secondary Schools*, HMSO.

11 The popular vocabulary of truancy

Dennis O'Keeffe

Introduction and summary

Mass education is an integral part of modernity. The modern world is inconceivable without elaborate schooling. But no human institutions work perfectly, and truancy in turn is an ineradicable aspect of mass education. Its causes are primarily curricular; but it also has definite, though thus far quite inadequately charted, connections with compulsion. Scholars of truancy working in languages which have highly developed formal vocabulary for truancy and its related phenomena, will be greatly advantaged compared with researchers using languages which do not. But the demotic language of truancy is also rich in explanatory potential, affording us persuasive insights into how school, attendance and truancy are perceived. The 'truancy demotic' of the English language, certainly in the context of research into truancy done in England, suggests quite clearly that there is no widespread alienation from school in this country.

Truancy and its languages: formal and demotic

There may be some link with the obdurate ineducability of the English-speaking peoples, but English is especially rich in words signifying undutiful absence from school or lessons. Not only does English possess a highly developed formal vocabulary for this activity; it also boasts an enormous demotic terminology covering the same phenomenon.

These vocabularies, formal and informal, correspond manifestly to a huge activity on the part of schoolchildren. The University of North London Truancy Unit has shown the worrying scale of truancy in England. Is there, then, a contradiction—between compulsory education and widespread truancy—at the heart of our educational arrangements? It is clear that no modern society can survive without elaborate institutions of teaching and learning. Yet huge numbers of teenagers truant. The tension seems less, however, in view of the evidence also uncovered by the Truancy Unit, to the effect that most teenage children, including most truants, actually approve of most of the curriculum and like school (O'Keeffe, 1994).

The appropriate conclusion is that school is not so much repudiated by its compulsorily detained clientèle, as rejected in varying part. This certainly seems to be the case in England. All we are really up against with this seeming contradiction is the well attested fact that human institutions do not function at Utopian levels.

The formal language

The formal vocabulary of unjustified absence when pupils are party to the act, is highly developed. Not only is 'truant' both noun and verb, but in the American case and increasingly in the British case too, it is a perfectly understood adjective as well, as in the expression 'the child is truant'. Moreover, there is also a related abstract noun of great force denoting the activity: 'truancy'. When truancy receives the proper attention it warrants from the sociologists and economists, those nations which pay attention will need a distinctive vocabulary to encompass the phenomenon.

There is very little well-known writing on compulsory education, which is the great unvoiced background issue for the study and understanding of truancy. The real advances will perhaps occur when some learned philosopher pens his or her thoughts on truants, truancy and compulsory attendance. At the very least this philosopher will need to write in a language which handles the central conceptual apparatus adequately. This English gives every promise of being able to do.

This promise certainly distinguishes English from the Latin languages. These have a very undeveloped formal vocabulary for truant and truancy. The French *'faire l'école buissonière'* (to make school in the bushes) is a cumbersome and inflexible verbal phrase, and not used much now anyway. It is not to be compared with the economy of the English verb 'truant', which gets there in one, as against the French four, and is more accurate to boot. (Who says truants go to the bushes and who says they 'do' school when they abscond?) The phrase is really only a clumsy demotic.

The French do have a neat demotic. They say 'sécher les cours' or 'sécher l'école'—'cutting' class or school as the British, and even more the Americans, say. The appropriate formal language is missing, however. There is a French noun 'truand'; but this means a beggar or vagrant, and carries undertones of criminality and waywardness, far beyond the normal range of meanings associated with our noun 'truant'. It is true that for some people in this country, senior British politicians included, the word 'truant' does summon up images of the deviant and the delinquent. But this is today contested. Most British researchers into truancy and attendance would probably disassociate themselves from any mechanistic connection. The University of North London Truancy Unit, for example, does not associate truancy automatically with anything untoward or antisocial.

This French word 'truand', as it happens, was in earlier centuries spelt 'truant', and, indeed, is from the same source as our 'truant'. This source is not, as the sound of the word might seem to indicate, mainstream French itself. The word 'truant' is not the present participle of a verb 'truer' to 'truant'. There is no such verb. It is of Celtic origin, with extant words in Irish. It is quite clear that French could do with reviving its ancient vocabulary. It could claim impeccable etymological grounds as well as explanatory functional ones for this and feel free to deny that it was creating a Franglais neologism.

There is, we have said, a demotic French covering the phenomena of truancy, and the demotic will greatly repay careful study in any language. But in terms of formal analysis the English language is advantaged by comparison, being quite simply much more flexible and richer than the French. These formal limitations also apply to other Latin languages. This contrasts with the Slavonic languages, which my sociological colleagues in Poland have assured me do have a formal vocabulary for truant and truancy.

Truancy and modernity

Truancy is a huge problem throughout the advanced western societies. Most of our American contacts, though the American research is not very developed, believe that truancy is far worse in the big American cities than in our British ones.[1] Preliminary considerations also strongly suggest that it is likely to be greater in France than in Great Britain. France's pastoral system is notoriously skeletal, and the intake to secondary schools is even more inadequately prepared than its English counterpart (Nemo, 1993).

Complex education systems are here to stay, though they need not be immutably fixed. It is perfectly conceivable, for example, that the schools of the future will be smaller and more intimate, as well as much more flexible, than the typical schools of the present. This may, and we can say no more, have a favourable impact on the willingness of the young to come to class. All human institutions, however, tend to produce both malfunctions and dysfunctions. The former means they do not do adequately what (the generality of) people expect from them. The latter means they do things which people do not want at all, do not consider objectively valid.

It is not clear to what extent truancy constitutes failure. Even if each act of truancy indicates failure in its own right—the lesson on offer, or in a minority of cases the school itself, appeals less than some other course of action—it does not follow that the outcome is all loss. It may be that a cheerful homeostasis has occurred and that psychological equilibrium has been restored. It is not certain, therefore, to what extent truancy can be connected with the failure of the educational venture. Is a high level of truancy analogous, for example, to a high level of divorce? Quite how does one index the success or failure of an institution? Divorce has not made marriage unpopular. Far from it. Nor is truancy associated with the unpopularity of school. School is, on the contrary, a very popular institution.

Malfunctions and dysfunctions may coincide. If, as is argued elsewhere in this volume, progressive education is largely dysfunctional, this dysfunctionality is also associated with the malfunctions of illiteracy, innumeracy and inadequate factual learning. Since, as the research by the Truancy Unit shows, truancy is mostly a curricular phenomenon, it is clear that it has strong, though as yet strictly indeterminate, links with educational malfunction and dysfunction.[2]

It is suggested elsewhere in this book that truancy can be reduced. It is Utopian to imagine that it could ever be eradicated. It is also unlikely that the compulsory education with which, however vaguely, it is associated, will be removed in the foreseeable future. Death, the taxes and compulsory school are on the agenda as far as the imagination can run. So, in smaller or larger versions, is truancy.

It has been suggested that a developed formal vocabulary on the subject of truancy will be of great use to the further study of a vast and enduring problem of modernity itself. In modern economies people have to be schooled. Some of them truant a lot of the time and most of them at least occasionally.[3] Since I also intimated that a study of slang usage in the same area might also pay dividends, let us now consider briefly the explanatory light which might be cast by analysis of a 'truancy demotic'.

Truancy and the demotic

I once gave a lecture on truancy to the Educational Social Workers of an LEA whose Director of Education rejoices in the name 'Bunker'. I was irresistibly drawn to making some gentle fun of this. 'Bunk off' and 'bunking' are the most common slang for truant and truancy in England, with the 'off' largely an optional extra. 'Does he bunk?' means the same as 'Does he bunk off?' In any event, 'bunk off' and its various combinations are known universally in the South of England and understood virtually everywhere in Britain. To pursue the pleasantry, 'Is Johnny a bunker?' would be widely understood as asking whether Johnny plays truant.

In the Midlands and North they also speak of 'wagging' and 'sagging', again with and without the 'off' in tow. I found when I was working in Australia that 'wagging' was the most common term for truancy there too. 'Dolling', 'skiving' and even 'slamming' are in use in England. Wales favours 'mitching', a term sometimes found in Ireland and the United States as well. British and American usages overlap at times. What we in Great Britain call post-registration truancy, is often called 'cutting class' in both countries. The Americans, however, also reduce this to 'cutting' and in addition, they speak of 'cutting school'. This is not common in Great Britain.

Americans also 'sluff' and 'ditch'. In England we find on Tyneside a particularly fetching combination. Since the word 'wife' in the local working-class dialect means any adult woman, any woman who works as an Educational Social Worker is likely to be referred to as the 'wag-wife'. The Welsh used to have a vivid term too, though I do not know if it is still used. At one time the truant officer in Wales was known as the 'whipper-in'. This last phrase testifies to the weak but real coercion associated, right from the start, at least for some children, with the whole business of compulsory education.

The 'weak' is an important word here. There may be children

who reject school with horror, hatred and revulsion. In the English case we did not find these attitudes common. A few of the questionnaires on our huge survey contained abuse and swear words, but only a few. The English demotic vocabulary of truancy is not one which resounds with alienation, with rejection of school as an institution, or with hatred of teachers.

A useful comparison is with the language surrounding the police. The police are sometimes regarded with moderate affection even by miscreants. 'Bill' and 'old Bill', 'cops', 'coppers' and 'the law': these are mild and good-natured terms. Their tone is comparable to 'bunking' or 'wagging'. The uglier 'filth' and 'pigs' tell a different story. Real hatred inheres in demotic vocabulary of this type. Strike-breakers are called 'scabs', prison-warders are referred to as 'screws' and there is the whole panoply of abusive terms used by people who hate others of different race.

There are in the British case no such widespread hate-laden terms for school and its officers. The gentle demotic vocabulary of truancy supports two of the central empirical claims of the University of North London Truancy Unit:

1. Truants more often than not like school.
2. There is no apparent, widespread, general alienation from compulsory education in English society.

'Bunking', 'wagging' and the rest, conjure up a good-natured game of wits between errant children and the institution seeking to confine them in some way. Such children may find school, more typically lessons, at the worst appalling. At best, and more usually, they may simply find compulsory attendance less interesting and enjoyable than some other beckoning prospect. This, we should remember, most typically does not even involve leaving the school building.

At the same time the sheer number of terms in use suggests that (effectively) compulsory attendance meets almost ubiquitous resistance from some quarters. This has probably always been so. Truancy is an ineradicable feature of compulsory education, it seems. Not that it hinges exclusively on compulsion. These is huge (though unresearched) truancy from colleges of further education, for example. Nevertheless, we can say that the requirement that teenage children be in class as and when school and the law says, has in all likelihood always been resisted, equally probably, for the main part rather good-naturedly. While it would require an elaborate social history to uncover the historical origins and precise connotation of the various demotic terms employed, none that I have ever come across is characterised by intractable hatred and contempt.

This is important. One of the central problems in social science and history is the difficulty of identifying the character of the phenomena being investigated. In the case of education, compulsory or otherwise, there is nothing like general agreement among the philosophers and social scientists involved, as to what the whole exercise is for.

Common language may provide some help. The demotic vocabulary which surrounds an activity may give us some clues as to the moral and affective outlooks of those who engage in it. The key to public understanding may reside in the slang used by the masses.

There are still people who discern a clear line from truanting to hanging about on street corners, to committing crime, to spending a life in and out of prison. If this is the case, it concerns only a small minority of truants. It is certainly not an opinion one would easily be led to by a consideration of the popular vocabulary for truancy. If truancy did mean protocriminality, loathing for school and all authority, a disposition to theft and violence, then such attitudes would surely be registered in our truancy demotic. At least to date, thank God, they are not.

Notes

1. For example, the leading American educationalist, Professor Bruce Cooper, of Fordham University.
2. The causes of truancy are overwhelmingly curricular. *See* O'Keeffe, op cit, Chapter 4.
3. Patricia Stoll's research into nine secondary schools, using a research time-base of 15/16 months, rather than the six-week one in O'Keeffe, op cit, found levels of up to 70 per cent *vis-à-vis* at least acts of occasional truancy. *See* Patricia Stoll and Dennis O'Keeffe (1989) *Officially Present: An Investigation into post-registration truancy in nine maintained schools*, Institute of Economic Affairs Education Unit.

References

Nemo, P. (1993) *Le Chaos Pédagogique*, Albin Michel.
O'Keeffe, D.J. (1994) *Truancy in English Secondary Schools*, HMSO.
Ibid, p. 71.

12 Truancy in the United States: a brief overview

Sean Gabb

Introduction

In looking at the present state of American research into truancy, it seems appropriate to turn Marx on his head: so far, educationalists have only tried to change the world in various ways—the point is to understand it.

During the past 15 years or so, much research has been done. Looking only to the journals, the literature is impressively bulky. Nevertheless, it seems fair to say that the great majority of truancy research—and therefore most truancy policy—has been conducted on the basis of two rival approaches, both of which are misconceived.

Empiricism—1

First, there is what for want of a better name will be called the 'empirical approach'. Now, this is not empiricism in the philosophical sense, which involves the framing of hypotheses and their testing by carefully structured research. It is, much rather, empiricism in the medical sense. It refers to the efforts of physicians in the early modern period to shake off the authority of the ancients. Galen, for example, had reasoned from the supposed nature of heat to the proper treatment of smallpox. Not surprisingly, many patients treated according to this method failed to recover. Reacting against it, physicians from the early sixteenth century tended to look for specific treatments that worked, and only later, if at all, asked why they worked.

For medical science, this kind of empiricism was a useful clearing of the ground, from which real progress could begin. But that is all it was. It has no place in the social sciences, where there are typically vast masses of data to be comprehended, and where the opportunities for tightly controlled experimentation are effectively zero.

And yet, this is the basic approach of many truancy researchers. They do not ask the three questions that in Great Britain are increasingly seen as crucial to an understanding of the subject: How many school students play truant? What kind of students play truant? Why do they play truant? (O'Keeffe, 1981, 1986, 1994; Stoll, 1989; Stoll and O'Keeffe, 1989). In fact, they do not seem very concerned to understand the subject at all. The aim of the truancy empiricists is to get truanting students back into school—never mind why they are absent in the first place, and sometimes never mind by what means they are got back into school.

Hence the 'Tulsa initiative', described by Kara Wilson (1993). Tulsa County in Oklahoma contains 16 school districts. Some while ago, vexed by high truancy rates, the authorities there decided to start enforcing the State law to compel attendance at school. The most persistent truants and their legal guardians were identified, and a series of prosecutions was started.

Paul Eastwold (1989) describes similar initiatives across the country as a whole. One school district is so vigorous in its enforcement of the compulsory attendance statutes that it threatens the parents of persistent truants with fines and imprisonment.

Even where the extreme sanction of the criminal justice system is not invoked, there has been a general trend in the US towards a tightening of school discipline for dealing with truancy. This usually involves the imposition of academic penalties. At Aurora High School in Colorado, for example, persistent truants are suspended from school, and occasional truants are required to catch up on the class work they have missed (Stine, 1990). In other places, truants can be punished by grade reduction and exclusion from higher grades, or even from final examinations.

It would be strange if in a country so generally litigious as the US these strong methods had not been challenged in the courts. In fact, they have, though so far only at the State level. Clifford P.

Hooker (1985) reviews 12 recent law cases testing the legality of academic penalties. He finds their use to be 'widespread and increasing'. He also finds that the courts are reluctant to intervene except where due process has been obviously breached by the authorities. School rules to impose academic penalties have most chance of being upheld in court if they meet these criteria:

1. The rules should be explicitly stated and should be made known well in advance to students.
2. Students should not be barred from sitting final examinations simply on account of persistent truancy.
3. Academic penalties should be confined to those offences that would also merit suspension from school.
4. Such school rules should not be enforced in a manner that is obviously unfair or arbitrary.

Nevertheless, despite their increasing popularity, academic penalties should not be seen as the preferred option of the authorities. It seems, after all, a strange response to children who are damaging their education by staying away from school, to punish them with further damage to their education—often by excluding them from school. And so, many other initiatives rely less on negative than on positive inducements to high and regular attendance.

Robert K. Callaghan (1986) describes an absentee attendance programme at a rural, lower middle-class, mostly white elementary school. Its 722 students had a history of high truancy, according to their teachers and the other relevant authorities. A group of 14 chronic truants was selected. These students were told that they were expected to attend school every day, and that their attendance would be closely monitored. Failure to attend would not be punished, but consistently high attendance would be rewarded. There was to be a 'special time awards day' every Friday, when rewards would include ice-cream parties, pizzas, picnics, swimming trips to the local lake, and so forth.

Other districts combine both approaches, punishing truancy and rewarding high attendance (Zweig et al., 1979; Duckworth, 1988; Dowdle, 1990). Still other districts take a largely technological approach. For an early but extreme instance of this, consider 'Hi. Your Kid Cut Class Today. At the Tone, ...' (1983):

> And you thought you'd tried every trick in the book to cut student absenteeism. You haven't. Now that computers have become an accepted feature in many schools' administrative offices, you might want to check out a new, computerized telephone system that six Chicago schools are using. Each of the schools has installed a machine that telephones parents to

alert them that their child was absent from school that day. The principal simply records a message on the machine, and the computer automatically dials parents at a specified hour, usually in the evening. The message goes something like this: "Good evening. I'm Tom Jones, principal of Central High School. I am calling to let you know that your child was absent from school today. Please call the attendance officer at 555–1212 tomorrow between 8 am and 2.30 pm to explain the absence." The machine can make 50 calls per hour. If no one answers the telephone at a student's home, the machine will try twice more. The next morning, a printout allows the attendance officer to see which parents received—and which ones missed—the calls.

Each machine costs approximately $7,800, but the Chicago School Board expected the machines to pay for themselves within 15 months. The article continues:

> That's because when school attendance improves—it's expected to go up approximately three per cent—schools will earn more state aid. After conducting a tryout last fall in two schools with especially high absenteeism, attendance increased from 78.8 per cent to 85.6 per cent.

Similar hopes were expressed by Kathy D. Tuck and Frieda N. Shimbuli (1988)—see also Richard DuFour (1983) and Thomas Jacobson (1985). Indeed, similar hopes and claims have been expressed in all the studies cited above. Put in place the right combination of sticks and carrots, add where possible the fruits of modern technology—and attendance ought surely to rise. In the Aurora study, for example (Stine, 1990), the use of academic penalties is said to have reduced truancies to less than 1.25 per cent. Similarly, the 'Tulsa initiative' is said to have scared 'hundreds of students' back to school (Wilson, 1993). Largely because they are said to work, the courts have tended to view academic penalties in a sympathetic light (Hooker, 1985).

Yet if these methods have been as successful as is often claimed, it is worth asking why there remains so much concern in the literature about truancy in American schools. The Chicago School Board is supposed to have shown how to reduce truancy by nearly seven per cent in 1983. But there is no evidence to suggest that truancy in Chicago is even one per cent lower today than it was 11 years ago. Nor do the various stick and carrot experiments seem to have produced a general improvement.

It is unlikely, bearing in mind the strength of concern about truancy, and the accessibility of the literature, that any of the cures projected since the early 1980s have been overlooked. It seems far more likely that the projectors of these cures have been mistaken. This is indicated by the evidence of 'The 15-Day Attendance Policy' (1990) at Mount Diablo in California. An academic penalties scheme was set up across the district in 1985–86, and this was monitored during the next four years. In some schools, attendance improved; in others, it actually worsened. During the whole four-year period, the district experienced a minimal improvement in average attendance rates; and these could be explained by other intervening causes.

The nature of the evidence for the cures discussed above will be left for the moment to one side. But supposing that there have been improvements, it is worth recalling that extraordinary efforts will often produce extraordinary results. If school students know that they are being closely watched, and that expensive systems of punishments and reward have been put in place above them, it is natural that their attendance levels will improve. But as soon as the fact, or novelty, of surveillance diminishes, so too will its effects.

It is, then, possible that the cures discussed above have had at least some of the beneficial results claimed for them, but that they do not add up to a solution to the problem of truancy. To continue the medical simile, the empirical approach may have had the same kind of local effect on truancy as aspirin has on a fever: and for a permanent, effective cure, we must either hope for a spontaneous change in the attendant circumstances, or seek an understanding of the problem before trying to solve it.

Curing the child

This brings us to the second of the two approaches. This will be termed the 'social-engineering approach'. Researchers here have the advantage of trying to understand why students play truant. That is, they ask the third of the three questions mentioned above. Their answer is that truancy is very often a symptom of other problems in the students. They stay away from school because their social backgrounds have left them ill-equipped to handle the demands placed on them at school—or even to appreciate the value of an education. Income, social class, ethnic origin, peer pressure, substances consumed, stability of family—these are all held to have a causal effect on truancy. Change or alleviate these, the argument goes, and there will be corresponding changes in the truancy rates. (*See* on these points Howard et al., 1986; Hagborg, 1989; Dreilinger, 1992.)

To this end, in some districts, enforcement of the compulsory attendance laws has changed out of recognition. Del Stover (1991) gives an impressionistic account of truancy policing in Baltimore and Los Angeles. Here, truancy officers have tended to become indistinguishable from social workers, as they try to resolve the problems of broken homes and drug abuse and so forth that are believed to keep students away from school.

In Chicago, a Truants' Alternative and Optional Education Program has been developed to provide these services on a formal basis (Brownlee et al., 1989). Its founding aims were to provide 'preventive, interventive, and remedial services to keep students from becoming chronic truants'. Counselling of truants and the provision of alternative—and perhaps more personally-suited—schemes of education, feature heavily in the programme.

For some researchers, indeed, truants are not merely unfortunate, or 'disadvantaged', but in some degree victims of an illness amenable to treatment. Amy Diebolt and Lisa Herlache (1991) believe in the usefulness of having school psychologists provide 'interventions for truancy'. These are to replace the 'predominantly punitive' and allegedly ineffectual methods of dealing with truancy. They discuss 'risk factors associated with truancy' just as if it were a physical disease in need of epidemiological investigation. Writing somewhat earlier, Meryl E. Englander (1986) discusses the possibilities of 'rehabilitating' individual truants with a 'diagnostic-treatment paradigm'—*see* also James H. LaGoy (1987).

In this respect, the American research shows broad similarities to the majority of recent British research, which has also tended to look to the backgrounds of school students for an explanation of their playing truant—e.g. Tyerman (1968), Hersov and Berg (1980), Reid (1986), and many others. In both cases, the starting assumption is of a deficiency in the student, which the authorities can investigate and in principle remedy.

However, as in Great Britain, and as with 'empiricism', this approach does not appear to have succeeded. Geraldine D. Brownlee et al. (1989) frankly confess that the Truants' Alternative and Optional Educational Program has not been a success. The findings of their study 'indicate that the proposed objectives have not been met'. This is partly ascribed to a funding reduction, but cannot be dismissed. It seems that the educational psychologist has been no more effective than the lawyer and the policeman in compelling attendance at school where there is no desire to attend.

Empiricism—2

As said, the social engineers have at least in principle an advantage over the empiricists thus far described, in so far as they ask *why* some school students play truant. If their approach also fails to deliver solid results, it is perhaps because they do not ask the two earlier questions mentioned above. As with Tyerman et al. in Great Britain, they have answered their one question by reasoning from three untested assumptions.

First, they have assumed that truancy rates can be accurately measured by counting the number of students not present at morning roll call ('Hi. Your Kid Cut Class Today. At the Tone, ...', 1983; Callaghan, 1986; Coleman, 1986; Tuck and Shimbuli, 1988; Stine, 1990).

Second, they have assumed that at least the majority of truanting students have the same 'problems of adjustment' as those who come to the attention of the courts and educational psychologists.

Third, they have assumed that what 'problems of adjustment' do exist proceed more from the unhappy backgrounds of the students than from any deficiencies on the part of the schools.

Each of these assumptions has been called seriously into question by the most recent British research (O'Keeffe, 1981, 1986, 1994; Stoll, 1989; Stoll and O'Keeffe, 1989). In Great Britain, truancy has been divided under two headings—'blanket', meaning unauthorised absences *from school*; and 'post-registration', meaning unauthorised absences *from certain lessons or groups of lessons*. The first sort is easily measured, since students are marked absent in a document which exists solely to detect absence. The second sort is far harder to measure, since students will normally have been marked officially present. The only reliable means of measurement are to go into the schools, and ask the students to fill in detailed questionnaires about their attendance habits and their reasons for non-attendance.

The consistent evidence of these questionnaires is that there is far more post-registration than blanket truancy; that both kinds of truancy are greatest in the last years of compulsory schooling; and that the great majority of post-registration truants do not have any of the 'problems of adjustment' that those truants who have so far featured most in the literature are said to have. According to Dennis J. O'Keeffe (*passim*), the majority of truanting students—of both kinds—go absent because they do not like certain lessons. If this is the case, the most obvious road to improvement lies not in counselling or rehabilitation—still less in punishment and reward—but in a reassessment of the school curriculum.

There is some recognition of all this in the American literature. See, for example, the Association of California School Administrators (1983):

Truancy sweeps, a cooperative effort of the high school district, Santa Maria Police Department, and Santa Barbara Sheriff's Department, gave us a valuable insight. The sweeps, unannounced to the public but coordinated by high school assistant principals and law enforcement agencies, were part of a concentrated effort to improve attendance. To our surprise, we found that the students who were picked up on these sweeps were not habitual trouble-makers or truants!

In the same year, David Brown (1983) expressed doubt regarding the role of individual or social pathologies as an explanation for truancy. He suggests looking instead at the contribution of the schools. Again, Josie Foehrenbach (1988) doubts if any scheme of truancy reduction can work that does not also improve the ability of schools to educate.

Then, most notably, there is the work of Kenneth Duckworth and John deJong (1986). In many respects, this echoes, and even predates, the work of Dennis O'Keeffe and Pat Stoll (*passim*). Six high schools in the north western States were studied during 1984 and 1985, to determine the variation of students' reports of the frequency with which they played both kinds of truancy—here called 'skipping school' and 'cutting class'. As in the British studies, data were collected directly from the students via questionnaires. Again, as in the British studies, truancy was at its greatest in the higher grades; and the main reason given for selective cutting was dislike of a particular class, or failure to have completed homework. There are other consistencies of findings between the studies that are most interesting.

Conclusion

Bearing in mind the scarcity of other truly empirical research into truancy in the US the Duckworth and deJong study is remarkable. Nevertheless, it lacks the large base of the British studies, and must be seen as evidence of what could be achieved were the resources made available.

Bibliography

Brown, D. (1983) 'Truants, Families and Schools: A Critique of the Literature on Truancy', *Educational Review*, vol. 35, no. 3.

Brownlee, G.D. et al. (1989) 'An Evaluation of Alternative Programs for High School Truants', a paper presented at the Annual Meeting of the American Educational Research Association.

Callaghan, R.K. (1986) *The Development and Implementation of an Absentee Improvement Program*, M.S. Practicum, Nova University.

Coleman, J.M. (1986) *Recommendations and Concerns Pertaining to Strategies for Improving Student Attendance and Reducing the Dropout Rate*, Cleveland Public Schools, Ohio.

Cox, C., Marks, J. and Pomian Srzednick, M. (1983) *Standards in English Schools*, National Council for Educational Standards.

Diebolt, A. and Herlache, L. (1991) 'The School Psychologist as a Consultant in Truancy Prevention', a paper presented at the Annual Meeting of the National Association of School Psychologists, Dallas.

Dowdle, J.M. (1990) 'Keeping Kids in School', *North Central Association Quarterly*, vol. 64, no. 2.

Dreilinger, M. (1992) *School Attendance, Truancy and Dropping Out*, Bureau for At-Risk Youth, New York.

Duckworth, K. (1988) 'Coping with Student Absenteeism', *The Practitioner*, National Association of Secondary School Principals, Virginia, vol. 14, no. 4.

Duckworth, K. and deJong, J. (1986) *Variation in Student Skipping: A Study of Six High Schools. Final Report*, Center for Educational Policy and Management, University of Oregon, Oregon.

DuFour, R. (1983) 'Crackdown on Attendance—The Word is Out', *NASSP Bulletin*, vol. 67, no. 464.

Eastwold, P. (1989) 'Attendance is Important: Combating Truancy in the Secondary School', *NASSP Bulletin*, vol. 73, no. 516.

Englander, M.E. (1986) 'Truancy/Self-Esteem', a paper presented at the Annual Meeting of the American Educational Research Association.

The 15-Day Attendance Policy: Final Evaluation (1990) the Mount Diablo Unified School District, Concord, California.

Foehrenbach, J. (1988) *Preparing for Learnfare: Setting the Conditions for a Questionable Experiment*, Center for Law and Social Policy, Washington DC.

Hagborg, W.J. (1989) 'A Study of Persistent Absenteeism and Severely Emotionally Disturbed Adolescents', *Behavioral Disorders*, vol. 15, no. 1.

Hersov, L. and Berg, I. (eds) (1980) *Out of School*, Chichester, John Wiley.

'Hi. Your Kid Cut Class Today. At the Tone, ...' (1983) *Executive Educator*, National School Boards Association, Washington D.C., vol. 5, no. 8.

Hooker, C.P. (1985) 'Academic Penalties for Student Misconduct', in Jones, T.N. and Semler, D.P. (eds), *School Law Update*, National Organization on Legal Problems of Education, Kansas.

Howard, R.C. et al. (1983) 'Factors Associated with Juvenile Detention Truancy', *Adolescence*, vol. 21, no. 82.

Jacobson, T. (1985) 'Increased Attendance Through Enhanced Communication', *Technological Horizons in Education*, vol. 12, no. 10.

LaGoy, J.H. (1987) *Improving Student Attendance and Achievement through Intervention of a Student Support/Home-School Liaison Committee*, EdD Thesis, Nova University.

Mortimore, P. (1988) *School Matters: the junior years*, Open Books.

Nemo, P. (1993) *Le Chaos Pédagogique*, Albin Michel.

O'Keeffe, D.J. (1981) 'Labour in Vain: Industry, Truancy and the School Curriculum', in Flew, A. (et al.), *The Pied Pipers of Education*, London, Social Affairs Unit.

O'Keeffe, D.J. (ed.) (1986) *The Wayward Curriculum*, London, Social Affairs Unit.

O'Keeffe, D.J. (1994) *Truancy in English Secondary Schools*, London, HMSO.

Reid, K. (1986) 'Truancy and School Absenteeism: The State of the Art', *Maladjustment and Therapeutic Education*, vol. 4, part 3.

Rood, R.E. (1989) 'Advice for Administrators: Writing the Attendance Policy', *NASSP Bulletin*, vol. 73, no. 516.

Rutter, Michael (1979) *Fifteen Thousand Hours*, Open Books.

Smith, D.J. and Thomlinson, S. (1989) *The School Effect: A Study of Multiracial Comprehensives*, Policy Studies Institute.

Stine, M.D. (1990) 'Do Your Students a Favor and Get Tough on Truants', *Executive Educator*, vol. 12, no. 3.

Stoll, P.A. (1989) *Post-Registration Truancy: A Study*, Thesis submitted to the Polytechnic of North London.

Stoll, P.A. and O'Keeffe, D.J. (1989) *Officially Present: An Investigation into Post-Registration Truancy in Nine Maintained Secondary Schools*, London, Institute of Economic Affairs.

Stover, D. (1991) 'Today's "Hooky Cops" are out to Save Troubled Parents', *Executive Educator*, vol. 13, no. 7.

Truancy Sweeps. Target Area: Discipline (1983) the Association of California School Administrators (ACSA) Task Force on Public Confidence.

Tuck, K.D. and Shimbuli, F.N. (1988) *An Evaluation of the Truancy Prevention Plan*, Washington DC, District of Columbia Public Schools.

Tyerman, M. (ed.) (1968) *Truancy*, London, University of London Press.

Willis, P. (1977) *Learning to Labour*, Saxon House.

Wilson, K.G. (1993) 'Tough on Truants', *American School Board Journal*, vol. 180, no. 4.

Zweig, John T. et al. (1979) 'The Contingent use of Trading Stamps in Reducing Truancy: A Case Report', *Journal of Experimental Education*, vol. 47, no. 3.

Index